The Evicted

John A. Oliver and Patricia L. Oliver

ISBN-10: 0692687955
ISBN-13: 978-0692687956

Dedication

This book is dedicated to all those warriors and their families who sacrifice so much for their country and beliefs. The agony and trauma continue and are never forgotten. We who are more fortunate are so appreciative of your service. Thank you.

Authors' Note

This book is a true, historical account of the atrocities of war and a personal account of how individuals and families are affected. It is not a story of man's godliness, but rather his struggles for survival and how God may choose to intervene at certain times in our lives.

The story is based on recollections and taped conversations with the individuals in the story, priceless memories furnished by members of the family, and encouragement from many people.

While the characters and the events are real, we do not attest to the absolute accuracy of some of their facts. As with all memories, there may be some inaccuracies. As closely as possible my wife and I have tried to portray the individuals truthfully with all their attributes and imperfections. In a few instances we have taken license to fill in gaps based on research and the best of our abilities.

A very special thanks goes to Mildred Sturmer—who first told me about this story and felt it was representative of the struggles of so many people—and to Kathy Hamel-Pleger for all her significant contributions. Many thanks to Greg Sturmer for his photos and suggestions. They were a blessing and without them the book would not be what it is.

Some years ago I was vacationing in San Francisco at Christmastime and left three years of interview tapes and all the paperwork for this story locked in my car. The next morning, I panicked when I found that all the story material had been stolen. All was gone. However, several days later, I received a message from my newspaper office that some man in San Francisco wanted me to call. It seems he had spotted some papers with my name on them in the back of a pickup and had taken the time to salvage them. They were water-soaked, but they were all there. Their miraculous return made my Christmas and helped me to bring the book to fruition. Thank you, Jim Hawkins. I am forever grateful to you. Without you, there would be no story.

John Oliver

The above was written by John Oliver prior to his demise in 2014.

5

Acknowledgements

I have completed The Evicted in keeping with a promise to John and the Sturmer family. It would not have been possible to do this to without the continual encouragement of Mildred Sturmer, my family, and many friends. Special thanks to those in my writing group: Marion Duckworth; Carolyn Wade; Carol Wilson; Linda Reinhardt; and Lidia Hu.

Thank you: Don Rifenbery, for all your support, time, and suggestions; Mark, Karen, and Kristin Sass; and Douglas Windom for your suggestions along the way. I am very grateful to Greg Sturmer who graciously allowed me to use his photo for the cover. So Beautiful.

Patricia Oliver

Part One:

Caught Between Two Worlds

A shuddering explosion rocked the ship jolting Roman from his upper berth with a certain fear that the *Empress Maria* was being attacked. He scrambled for his clothes as a cry rolled along the passage way outside his cabin, "A Zeppelin has attacked us!" Struggling into pants, shoes and his greatcoat, he stumbled up to the deck to witness the most unbelievable of scenes.

Flame-filled smoke rose like a pillar several hundred feet into the air from the forward section of the ship. Roman couldn't take it all in—nor did he want to. The damage overwhelmed his understanding. This destruction around him was his beloved *Empress Maria*, the newest and biggest ship of the Russian navy, pride of the Black Sea fleet.

I've only had a few weeks of sea duty aboard her. And now she's sinking alongside a pier right in her own home harbor of Sevastopol...not even from a battle at sea! Roman turned away from the crushing thought, his eyes moist.

Crew members struggled past, badly burned—limping or crawling. Roman quickly moved to help drag them farther back on the deck away from the terribly damaged areas. More explosions erupted, with mind-numbing regularity, which told Roman that the below- deck powder magazines were blowing. The magazine serving the Number One 12-inch gun turret collapsed, shooting its weapon into the air and dropping it back down on deck, a mass of fractured steel.

Roman staggered across the deck to the *Maria's* port side. He barely paid attention to the urgent cry, "Abandon ship! Abandon ship!"

Roman thought of his precious treasure in his cabin and resigned himself to the loss of the last connection to his grandfather.

Already many of the ship's higher-ranking officers were pushing and crowding in an attempt to escape. Knowing every moment counted, Roman clambered over the railing to the side of the hull, now upright, as the ship continued capsizing. His strategy didn't work. He slipped and tripped, toppling down the bruising jagged surface shredding his clothes and catapulting head first into the keel and on into the churning waters. Unconscious, he rolled into the debris of the exploding, flamed-filled waters.

Chapter 1

1914

The vast Moscow railroad station teemed with endless activity as the crowd bordered on being out of control. In the overcrowded station there was the cloying odor of sweat and unwashed bodies. Hunger draped the haggard features of young peasants swarming the station area. Many were in homespun shirts tied at the waist with a cord, pants stuffed into worn boots. Others were in ragtag uniforms—all in route to or from army camps. Their possessions were wrapped in long rolls flung over their shoulders. Chaos filled the station.

Elitists in officer's uniforms—trying to remain removed from the unruly masses—stood straight, arrogant, appearing in control of their surroundings: Most of them were going to war. There seemed to be no organization.

Restless, agitated movements kept people shifting like whirlpools in a stream. Unrest had been growing since the first sounds of war were echoed at the beginning of August. But they had escalated startlingly in the two weeks since the Russian mobilization efforts accelerated. Outside the station, streets were jammed with horse-drawn wagons and heavily laden trucks attempting to get to the freight yards with loads of military supplies.

The young man in the dark suit seemed out of place as the restless crowd pushed against him. He set his two suitcases down by a post and mopped his brow, then paused to get his bearings as he searched for his family in this crush of humanity. He looked agitated. *Why can't they keep up with me? They could get lost in this explosive mess. My train is due to depart.*

Despite his obvious irritation, Roman Sturmer radiated a look of anticipation and inner joy even as his eyes continued to frantically search the crowd. Just short of six feet tall, broad shouldered and barrel-chested, he had a high forehead above deep-set eyes and a strong, straight nose; but it was his mouth, wide with generous lips, that set his serious expression. *What is happening to my beloved Russia?*

At last he was on his way, but the excitement of pursuing his dream was somewhat dimmed by his family's displeasure at his choice: the romance of the sea over their military tradition.

Where's my family? Roman's eyes continued searching the crowds thinking that his mother, two brothers and a sister should have been immediately behind him just as he had cautioned. In this hectic movement a person could be a mere twenty feet from a family member and be invisible. His sigh registered both anxiety and irritation: time was fleeting. He hadn't even located the train for St. Petersburg and already his family was lost! *I can't miss the train.*

On this mid-August day, families—the more affluent—were still traveling to favorite vacation spots. Children were among the crush, unhappy down among the hips and knees of the adults; chaos or not. Russians had to move through Moscow to arrive from, or go anywhere. This city of many millions was Russia's railroad hub. Tracks branched out from here in all directions.

At last a cry of "Roman!" caught his attention and with it the lunging body of his youngest brother, George, threw his arms around one of Roman's legs, gripping it tightly. Roman's other brother, Oleg, his sister, Kira, and his mother, Inna, rushed toward him. His mother was a pretty, fashionably dressed woman, seemingly out of place in the throng. People moved aside as she passed, and turned around to stare admiringly.

"Roman!" she called. "Thank God you waited. We tried to keep up, but you moved too fast."

"But Mother"—the young man began but was interrupted.

"—I know. You have a train to catch." She smiled up at him. "Well, let's hurry then."

As he stooped to pick up his suitcases, his mother thrust one arm through his and marched staunchly beside him seemingly unbothered by the surroundings. While his siblings struggled to keep up, Roman searched intently for the proper train track. In doing, so he came face to face with another of the posters emblazoned with the blood red call to arms, "Fight for Russia!" Such reminders were everywhere: "Join the War!" Roman felt separated from that call, isolated: he wasn't emotionally carried away with it.

His destination was not the Army. The thought of *his* destination brought excitement. The journey to St. Petersburg was another step towards fulfilling Roman's dream of joining the Imperial Russian Navy—the dream he'd held from childhood.

Roman spotted the right track and urged his family to the waiting train. His mother fussed with his suit lapel; touched his hair; and reached up to kiss his cheek while the children ogled the train. Big as he was, he was still her little boy. He was patient and dutiful but anxious to board the train. As the family hesitated in saying their goodbyes, the train's whistle screeched a warning. Roman hastened aboard and found a compartment with room for one more passenger. He stored his luggage and stuck his head outside hoping for one last glimpse of his family. As he spotted them in the forest of people smiling bravely, he waved his last goodbye.

A sudden jolt forced Roman into his seat. The St. Petersburg-bound train jerked as it slowly chugged out of the station.

Steadily, the train increased its speed making its way along the almost endless network of rails in the Moscow yards. Eventually the city thinned out after passing clusters of dirty industrial buildings. Gradually, open spaces increased between the crude shanties clustered camp-like alongside the tracks. At last the train chugged past open fields and wooded areas gradually gaining speed as it crossed a great plain with rolling hills rising and falling between flat lands.

Roman briefly nodded courteously to his fellow passengers: as he sank into the kind of hypnotic drowsiness that afflicts travelers lulled by the rhythmic clacking of the wheels on the track, he became aware of just what this separation from his family meant. He was really alone. He was on his own, aware of his aloneness.

Secluded in his thoughts, memories of childhood paraded by in startling clarity. They had been coming on unbidden for the last several days, as if to emphasize this drastic change in his life. Only 18 years old, Roman was a man now, in every way but experience. He was on his way to the naval academy.

Chapter 2

Roman leaned back in his seat, annoyed with the ongoing interruptions of the erratic train motions and the restless passengers settling themselves near him. As he relaxed, he began to think of his early youth and the family life he was leaving behind. Yes, he would miss it. But his vivid memories and pictures of Gdansk, Poland, where they'd gone in 1905 on his ninth birthday overruled other thoughts—as they often did.

Great German warships gathered in Poland's Gdansk harbor on the Baltic Sea, mesmerizing him as he stood on the dock. He'd never seen anything so huge or so enthralling. From a distance, officers patrolling the decks looked like ants to the small boy. In his mind, from the instant his eyes had spied the visiting fleet, he was aboard the flagship—0—walking along the deck, dwarfed by the great guns and the bulwarks of the turrets and the towering superstructures. His ship: Mysterious, powerful beyond measure, a beautiful hulking presence that seemed to protect him and frighten him at the same time. This German fleet is beyond anything Russia had at sea, it seemed to him. It defied all imagination. How could men build such gigantic things? How could they stay afloat? With all that steel, why didn't they just sink to the bottom of the sea?

He'd stood fixated, not ready to leave, while his mother, sister and both of his brothers walked on until they'd come back to pull him out of his trance. "Come, Roman, we're ready to leave."

At home in Warsaw, Roman had read about Russia's great warships, but he recalled—all too vividly—that when he'd enthusiastically told of his plans to serve at sea, his father and grandfather were stunned and asked him, "How can you even think of being a naval officer! What about family tradition?" Both men were career Russian Army officers and proud of it. An army career was one of the identifying characteristics of his family going back years to their heritage in Nizhnyy-Novgorod on the Volga River. Yet, despite their disappointment, they encouraged him to think for himself.

The main focus for the family during much of Roman's childhood revolved around army life as well as stories of the famous Volga farming region. His father, Arcady Andreyevich Sturmer, was an Army captain and later a colonel, an aide to the General in command of a regiment stationed just outside Warsaw (to dispel any attempted uprising while Warsaw was still part of the Russian Empire). When still a captain, he married Inna Kazimirovna Nasarjhevsky, the only daughter of Lieutenant General Kazimir Dominikovich Nasarjhevsky.

Roman loved Warsaw. He spent most of his early childhood there, although he was born in a smaller town near there, Nova Alexandria, on August 23, 1896.

When Roman was eight-years-old, the family moved into a nine-room apartment on the third floor of a building in Warsaw near the Saxon Square. It was considered a luxurious apartment near the St. Alexander Nevsky Russian Orthodox Cathedral under construction in the square. Curiosity led to spending many hours watching workmen as they laboriously worked constructing the beautiful church. At that time, it would be the tallest building in Warsaw, 70 meters (about 227 feet). Eventually it would feature 16 beautiful mosaic panels done by two Russian artists.

Roman continued with his thoughts, thinking about that fine home. It was spacious with everything on one floor—dining room, parlor, kitchen and bedrooms. *It's comfortable,* he thought as he reminisced. *In the front is my parents' bedroom and one for the smallest children. Lucky Kira, two years younger than me, has a bedroom of her own down the hall. Even father has a separate study and a special desk. I loved to prepare my homework there.*

The large Sturmer apartment was furnished with typical middle class furnishings of the times. Large portraits in gilded frames hung artfully on the walls above glass-doored, wooden bookcases filled with classic books. Dark cabinets and dark furniture with curved backs softened by tufted somber fabrics filled the rooms.

Roman chuckled to himself, *I didn't even have a bedroom to myself so I had to sleep in my parents' room when they entertained. I spent a lot of time sleeping on the couch in the living room after everyone left at 4 o'clock in the morning after a party. They didn't know that I could hear the conversations as I crept out of their bedroom before everyone left. But, it was a happy time.*

In 1904, after Roman's grandmother died, his grandfather came to live with the family in their new apartment. Roman considered his grandfather's (*Dedushka's*) room the best place in the whole apartment: he considered it was the happiest place for him.

Roman's mother was the caretaker of the family finances. As his Army pension, *Dedushka* Kazimir, received 500 rubles a month, which enabled the family to live far better than only on Colonel Sturmer's salary of 250 rubles.

Roman settled more comfortably in his train seat, closed his eyes again, reviewing more of his earlier years. *Father and grandfather each got paid on the 20th of the month. Grandfather would go to the government bank and bring 500 rubles home to his mother, Inna. About half past three, father would come home and bring Inna his 250 ruble in gold. Mother grabbed the money and went to a special table that she'd then open. Then she put all those gold pieces into a drawer, put down the cover, and locked them up—except for the ones she allotted to father and grandfather!*

Roman had been both frustrated and fascinated with the money ritual. He later learned that his mother would only give his father three rubles a month for a shave and a haircut! A shave cost about 20 kopeks and a haircut was about two kopeks. Roman had observed that those three rubles would suffice his father's needs for a whole month: a beard and mustache trim which Roman thought made him look like the pictures of Kaiser Wilhelm of Germany.

A kopek was worth about half a cent. At the time $1 was equal to two rubles and there were 100 kopeks in a ruble."

Those kopeks and rubles also played an important role in Roman's relationship with his *Dedushka* Kazimir. *He was very fond of me,* Roman remembered. *I loved being his pet! Oh! He just loved me! And it cost him 50 kopeks a day! Each time I went into his room—every day—I just dipped into his wallet. It was a game between us. I loved it when he took me captive.*

"Aha! I've caught you this time!" *Dedushka* would growl and grab Roman in a bear hug. Then they would both laugh uproariously. Roman saved the pilfered kopeks in a little box, and eventually he accumulated 250 rubles, a considerable treasure. That tiny treasure chest was an important part of home to him and he carried it with him wherever he went.

Roman looked back on his young years as special and one of the best times of his life. His mother used to say, "I wish Time would stop." It was a happy time for the family and they often spoke of their origins. His mother was Russian and his father, German. The Sturmer family originated somewhere in the genealogical eras of Germany, but eventually surfaced—as did many German families along with other Europeans—who initially were invited by Catherine the Great to immigrate and farm the Russian Volga region while maintaining their own language and culture.

Roman was curious about the Volga region and Nizhny Novgorod in particular. He found it exciting and frequently asked his parents and grandfather a lot of questions. "How old is it and why are we so proud of it? What makes it famous?"

"Well, son, it was founded in 1221 and eventually became significant because it was at the intersection of Russia's developing main east-west trade route. It was also a target for marauders, so for years it was surrounded by a moat and centered in a wooden kremlin, or citadel," his father told him. "It was ravaged and burned seven times by Tatar tribes and armies, but Nizhny Novgorod rebuilt many times."

Roman persisted with more questions. "But why is it famous now?" He was forever asking questions.

Grandfather said, "It was so successful against invading enemies and as a trade center that it grew into a renowned crafts and cultural hub and later became the capital of the region."

Roman also learned it had become renowned for making the sails for the ships that founded the Russian navy. Thus, it became more significant to him. He learned that at one time the city made about half of all Russian ships; and the first motorized ships in the world were manufactured there. That excited him.

During the years following the visit to Gdansk, the memory of those magnificent battleships remained hypnotic and beckoned Roman. On more nights than he could count as he dropped off to sleep, he envisioned himself aboard one of them, proudly walking the decks in his naval uniform. He often wished he could share his dream with his father and grandfather. In his heart he always knew that one day he definitely would answer the call of the sea, but he'd always known it would not be without intense opposition.

Gradually the train made a noticeable descent to the marshlands where Peter the Great's tiny hut had grown into the great city of St. Petersburg with its stunning system of canals and waterways.

The Great Fair at Nizhny Novgorod

Everyone loves a fair, especially the vendors. Nizhny Novgorod, situated at the junction of the Volga and Oka rivers, was home to a great fair each summer. In the early 1900's it was reputed to bring in approximately 400,000 traders and goods valued at $120,000,000. The fair was a continuation of one begun so many years ago and had been in Nizhny-Novgorod since 1817.

Goods and traders, visitors and residents traveled to the Russian fair from all over Europe and Asia, mostly by steamers or by railway. From America and Europe, from the Russian shores of the Caspian and Black Seas, this fair united people. People could be seen observing the merchandise as it was being unloaded from steamers on the Volga by Tartar laborers on the nearly 10-mile long wharves of Nizhny Novgorod.

There were iron products from Tula, an area near Moscow, and specialty products from many regions including precious stones and furs from Siberia and Central Asia. There were perfumes and spices, minerals and natural products, Swiss clocks and wooden gifts. Toys made by peasants, cotton goods and silks, ornaments, beautiful carpets, and dried food items were part of the offerings. From China came tea. Some vendors advertised their wares by stacking them in such a way to make their "booths". There were special quarters for each of the various types of offerings.

The normally quiet area became an enormous city of shops. Wherever one looked there were displays, bazaars, and shops. Were the buildings typical ones associated with fairs, canvas, ropes and flimsy materials? No. The annual event was so important that there were regular houses and large shops complete with sleeping quarters for the merchants and their servants. There were churches, hospitals, bars and theaters. Military posts kept down rioting throughout the town and area. From morning to night crowds of mingling people, carriages and wagons filled the streets. The bustle and activity was said to be unequalled in Europe. The sun rose at about four o'clock and already talking, bargaining and arguing filled the air. This was such a famous fair, that writers of the times, including Jules Verne, mentioned it in their writings.

Chapter 3

Roman's father was absent so often on military duty that Roman's mother was largely responsible for most family matters—education, discipline, family well-being, oversight of servants: the cook, a maid, and a governess. In the scheme of Russian society, the family was wealthy; not nobility, but definitely among the privileged.

Mother Inna made an excellent taskmaster and teacher. The Russian Orthodox Church had its official educational requirements, but she taught her children a great deal before they were even in school. She taught them arithmetic so that at an early age they knew enough to account for all the money that the cook spent at the market. *She* set the guidelines.

Under their mother's watchful eyes, the children learned Polish, Bulgarian, French, German and English—in addition to Russian. At mealtimes, for instance, the family spoke only the language of that particular day. If the children didn't speak in that day's language when asking for food, they didn't eat. Roman's love of food overcame his distaste for those studies, so he learned very well the language of each day.

Roman was a lazy student, largely from boredom. So he preferred to create his own studies when he could get away with it. As a child, he delighted in watching people outside the apartment, down on the plaza below. It gave him a strange delight. He loved music from an early age and liked to play march music on the phonograph setting the rhythm of the music in time to people's walk. Impishly he would play the music loud, hoping they could hear it on the street and wave to him. That lasted until his mother said, "That's enough!"

It was the custom in Russia that when old enough to attend the

Orthodox school, the children went to one building which housed elementary school, junior high and gymnasium (the equivalent of high school), for all their years. After four years of study, students got a kind of certificate which allowed them to teach younger children.

Considerable controversy arose between *Dedushka* Kashmir and his daughter over whether or not Roman would attend the Orthodox school. The old general was stubborn and wanted Roman with him all the time. He was used to people obeying him so, when Roman grew old enough for school, he told his grandson, "No. You stay at home with me. You don't need to go to school. After all," he boasted, "I taught your mother as a child, and look at her. She was fine without school." He argued that she, with his help, could teach the boy all he needed to know without the priests' and nuns' help.

Mother Inna ruled.

Roman went to school.

Grandfather was depressed.

Going to school had its joys for Roman, although not necessarily in the classroom. When his father would take Roman to school, the Polish people would call them '*Samovar* and *Embrycheck*' (Polish for teapot). His father was Samovar and Roman was Teapot. People said they resembled each other. Both were considered fat.

Roman loved his father and loved being with him. He considered him to be a wonderful man. He was fat, jolly, and of very good character. He never smoked. He was generally with many friends who would entertain him—almost every night—and then invite him to have dinner with them. But he would be on time for dinner at home. and kiss the children. Roman thought his smell, a "wonderful ambry", was the aroma of entertainment.

In 1905, a man came to see Roman's father and asked for his help. He said he was Cook No. 1 on a steamboat that traveled on the Vistula River from Warsaw to the German border and up to the Austrian border. The name of that boat was something that Roman thought sounded like *Panta Deos*. The man's name was Vicente Domanski and the family blamed his delicious food for making them fat.

Roman thought a lot about the family cook. *The first time I saw him: he was in our own kitchen preparing our dinner! Father had drafted him as his orderly. So, he became the orderly of Captain Sturmer in Warsaw and our cook. Oh boy! I never dreamed I would eat like I did or to have such food in our house. I ate things I never ate before. No wonder I'm fat!*

Saint Petersburg

St. Petersburg (called Petrograd between 1914 and 1924), the beautiful city created by Peter the Great to Russianize the swampy Baltic region, escalated from the swamps to a city built on pilings on islands of the Neva River. Conscripted peasants and Swedish prisoners of war built the foundations as canals were drained, transforming it into the "Venice of the North" so named as it appeared to be a city floating on water. In 1712, it was designated the capital of Russia. Libraries, museums, churches, palaces, fortresses and homes soon appeared once the land was drained. Nearby forests and plains produced a large trade in timber, tar, hemp, sugar and beetroot for St. Petersburg.

In the 1800's, majestic structures were built or elegantly renovated. The great St. Isaac's Cathedral with its golden domes was completed in 1858 after forty yeas of construction. An old saying claimed St. Petersburg was the head of Russia, Moscow the heart, and Nizhny-Novgorod the pocket.

The picturesque Winter Palace, built between 1754 and 1762, graces the northern side of Palace Square, and the nearby Admiralty building, topped by its famous gilded spire , is an example of Russian Empire style,. That spire remains one of St. Petersburg's main focal points and the center for naval activity.

In 1850, the first permanent bridge replaced pontoon bridges across the Neva River. Deeply frozen waterways were so strong that carriages and horse-drawn sleighs with tinkling bells carried the rich over the ice and along Nevski Prospekt, St. Petersburg's grand three-mile-long street. Even when the intense cold and wind of fall and winter penetrated St. Petersburg, warmly dressed shoppers and sightseers strolled along the boulevard while horse-drawn trams traveled down a center track. Gas lights illuminated the street.

Lined with banks, company offices, and many fine shops this street soon became known as one of the most elegant avenues in Europe. St. Petersburg was a city of endless art and religious treasures and churches. Alexander Dumas, the French writer once called it "the street of religious tolerance" because of the many churches of different denominations built along this broad boulevard.

The Admiralty,
St. Petersburg

Photo by Greg Sturmer

Chapter 4

"St. Petersburg," announced the porter rousing Roman from his childhood reverie. Excited, he hastened to get off as soon as the train came to a full stop. He collected his suitcases, stepped from the train and immediately flagged down a carriage. "To the Admiralty, please," he declared proudly trying not to appear too nervous.

At last! I'm finally at the Naval Academy. Is this really happening?

Roman had to blink his eyes. He had trouble believing he was actually standing here, at the end of Nevsky Prospekt; but the famed golden spire rose majestically before him over the Academy complex on Admiralty Island. *Yes, I'm really here.*

Roman dropped his suitcases beside him and just stood staring. He hadn't moved since he'd paid the carriage driver who had brought him from the train station. On this warm August day in 1914, Roman felt this was all he had dreamt of for so long. This day would mark the beginning of his career in the Russian Imperial Navy—hopefully a long one.

As he stood there looking, he had a quick flashback to the night months before this trip just prior to taking his entrance exams. His father had long ago relented of any disappointment over Roman's choice to join the navy instead of the army. He even insisted on accompanying Roman to St. Petersburg at an earlier time to cheer him on. His father had tried so hard to coax him into going to some of the nightclubs the evening before the exams, to relax from the stress he had built up within himself. He had declined the first several times his father persisted, but Roman finally gave in to please his father. Their evening together went fine until the girls came on stage for the dance troupe finale. Roman then wearily begged off, telling his father he needed to study a couple of things before going to bed. He needed the sleep before the following day's exams. He was more interested in his exams than in girls.

Roman's efforts paid off: he placed eighth out of 450 students applying to the Academy.

He stared at the Admiralty's magnificent building surrounded with its beautiful landscaping and the famed spire. Beyond were the government buildings and the Peter and Paul fortress. On the Finnish Gulf were the Kronstadt Fortress, and the palaces of the Czar Nicholas. The fortresses marked the outline of the city.

And now, here I am! I'm standing at the center of St. Petersburg, actually the very center of all Russia, just as Peter the Great had planned it two centuries ago. This brought Roman back from his memories.

Roman stood where Peter the Great had built his tiny log residence planning to construct ships that would form the navy's beginning. The exterior of his log building was covered with stone to fit in with his dream of building grand stone structures nearby. In Roman's mind the building of the beautiful city deserved special recognition.

Three of St. Petersburg's major avenues radiated out from this center—the broad, elegant, three-mile-long Nevsky Prospekt, the Median Prospekt, and Voznesensky Prospekt. Many of Russia's famed architects and builders had their hands in the construction of this city.

Truly, St. Petersburg deserves to be the capital of Russia. Roman stood transfixed, just as he had as a boy in Poland when he'd first seen the great warships of Germany's visiting fleet in Gdansk. He thought, *Could there be any city more beautiful in the world than this?*

He finally picked up his suitcases and headed toward the Admiralty buildings.

For him, a career in the Imperial Russian Navy was the most honorable of all careers. He knew that whatever honors would come to him would come through long, hard work.

Roman began his training with the same wide-eyed innocence and idealism of the other 18-year-old young men entering the Academy.

The rigorous training seemed endless. From morning to nightfall Roman studied: the math required for navigation; the clumsy, but eventually skillful, use of a sextant; learning the feel of a ship's rhythm under his feet; and mastering the motion and rigor of maneuvering a craft of thousands of tons so that it sidled up to a pier instead of crashing into it. At night he fell into bed, exhausted.

Roman became accustomed to weeks at sea on the training ship *Aurora*, which took him to all the Baltic ports under Russian governance—Latvia, Estonia, Finland—and seas beyond; places he'd only dreamed about. He endured the long rail trip to far-off Vladivostok, half a world away, on the Trans-Siberian Railway. In the best of weather conditions, it was a twelve-day trip through the frozen land. But, Roman loved all of it.

The Imperial Russian Naval Academy was noted as an elite institution, with a proud history harking back to a notorious early beginning. From that passion came Peter's great plan to make the Baltic Sea, the Russian Sea, safe from all invaders. Roman truly identified with the Czar's love of the sea and all that pertained to it.

> *The **Aurora** became renowned when it would fire blanks at the Winter Palace to signal storming of it during the Bolshevik Revolution in 1917.*
>
> *Later, the Aurora was to be preserved in St. Petersburg as a museum, an icon of that period.*

The Admiralty, and the area around, became the ship manufacturing center of the nation, and from that the navies that followed. Many of the students who came to the Academy had passion similar to Roman's, but none had more. Students were drawn mostly from families with a military tradition, largely naval of course, or from other segments of the aristocracy.

Education at the Academy was a combination of academic studies paired with practical application, theory and field work. The routine of grueling hours of study in addition to weeks at sea, required endurance. Roman had one goal and diligently adhered to it: he had to become a seaman before becoming a ship's officer.

Officer training at the Naval Academy was usually a four-year affair, but Roman and other students arriving in this year of 1914 would soon find the period would be shortened to two years because of the Great War with Germany.

For several months, Roman's Baltic Sea training was aboard the cruiser *Aurora*.

"Training is rigorous," Roman wrote to his family. "Our whole class, had to go to sea on one of the sailing vessels for training. I nearly flunked out because of my weight: I wasn't agile enough so I went on a herring diet and lost the excess weight. The other students have nicknamed me 'Mooha' (fly)".

Humor was often a break from the strenuous academic life of the students. Daily life was not all pomp, study, and formality. Even though Roman's classmates often teased him about always having his nose in a book instead of on the pretty girls, he loved to join in the fun.

The academy's students, including Roman, were no different from the mischievous youngsters who troubled other faculties. Professors were, after all, human beings underneath their authoritarian manners and students loved to find their idiosyncrasies. One professor revered the huge, magnificent compass made of inlaid wood on the floor in the center of the great entrance hall of the administrative building. He would always go around the columns lining the hall in order to get to the corridor beyond. When the students asked him why he didn't simply walk across the compass in the center, he replied, "That compass has paid my living for 40 years. Why should I step on it?"

Instead of admiring the professor's respect for the compass, his admission gave the students an idea of how to keep the professor from teaching his class. They chalked a compass in the entrance to his classroom. When the professor arrived, he would spot the compass and take a few steps backward. Then he would run and jump across the compass into the room. This trick became so popular that compasses appeared in the doorways of all the classrooms. Soon the poor professor was jumping hither and yon into whatever room he needed to be.

The tricks were not without repercussions. "One day the school's inspector saw the professor jumping and wondered why," Roman wrote. "When he saw the compass, he knew the cause immediately, and followed the professor into the classroom."

"Who is the midshipman on duty here?" Roman said the inspector asked.

When the student responsible came forward the inspector confined him to the brig for five days.

"Another professor hated boots," Roman wrote as he shared their pranks with his family. "One day students chalked a boot on the blackboard. When the professor came and saw the boot, he flew into a rage and began throwing chalk at it. The same building inspector happened by and saw this demonstration. Glaring at the students, he once again asked, 'Who's the midshipman on duty?' He pointed to the guilty one and said, 'You are confined to the brig for five days.'" Another prank died in infamy.

"Oh, but then there were the roosters!" Roman wrote as he continued the story.

"The rooster affair caused the greatest consternation of all. A professor took offense at five paper roosters a student had folded and placed on his desk. He grabbed them and crumpled them and threw them in the wastebasket. The next day there were 200 roosters in the room. The professor took longer, but eventually gathered them all up and destroyed them."

Roman chuckled to himself as he continued writing, "The next day 600 roosters appeared in the room. On the following day, 2,000 of the birds cluttered the room. Students had stayed up all night folding paper roosters. They were on the window ledges, on the chalk trays, on students' desks, all over the room!"

"The tireless inspector also discovered this mass impishness. However, this time, he confined not just one of us, but five midshipmen to the brig, and not for just five days, but 15 days. That unwelcome justice killed an untold number of our other pranks waiting in the wings."

Roman's two years at the Academy were not spent solely in rigorous studies and mischievous student pranks. He loved the special Russian holidays, particularly Easter. It was a time when Spring was in the air and nature was beginning to show the early signs of warmer weather. He looked forward to a time of quiet and relaxation—but it was not to be.

The *Aurora*, Roman's Training Ship

Picture by Greg Sturmer

The Russian Easter Basket

The Easter Basket of the Russian Orthodox Church is actually taken to church to be blessed and the dyed eggs consecrated. But, it is not the Easter basket generally associated with the holiday: There is no Easter Bunny. It is now a spiritual observance honoring Christ and His Resurrection culminating the 40-day Lenten fast before Easter which traditionally begins the Monday following Maslenitsa during which there has been much merry-making. "Blini Sunday" (blinis are like Russian crepes) begins Lent.

The typical Lent Fast of the Russian Orthodox eliminates all meat, eggs, dairy products, sugar, and other rich foods for the entire period. The end of Lent is then celebrated with a final Easter service (although others may follow) meant to enhance fellowship with other Christians and honor the resurrection of Jesus Christ in a festive manner. As the worship service begins at midnight with parishioners inside a darkened church, representative of the tomb from which Christ arose, they are then given a candle and go outside and walk in a circle with their lit candles praising the Lord. When the priest has knocked three times at the tomb door, it is finally opened for them to return, but now they enter a bright interior representing the Risen Lord. When the worship service ends, traditionally at 3:00 a.m., the potluck begins with everyone sharing their baskets and their joy.

The priest blesses the food and eggs in the baskets with holy water and ask that the Christians be truly thankful for what they are about to receive, and to recognize the presence of Christ and the Holy Spirit at the forthcoming meal.

Parishioners usually prepare the foods for family-sized baskets on Easter Eve. The baskets are filled with their offerings representative of foods given up and the traditional paskha meaning "Easter"—a sort of cheesecake dessert meant to be spread on kulich — a festive sweet yeast bread, and eggs—mainly red to represent the blood of Christ. The eggs are often given ceremonially by the priest or by friends one to another with a special Easter greeting.

Some eggs are fabulous works of art, such as those of Karl Faberge, first commissioned in 1884 by Czar Alexander III as a special Easter present for his wife.

Chapter 5

It was the Easter vacation of 1916 with its many special traditions. Roman stretched out his long legs as he struggled to get comfortable on the train trip to Moscow. His father had been transferred there from Warsaw after Roman had begun his studies at the academy. He was anxious to see the family and the new apartment. And, he especially looked forward to the food and relaxed hours of study—in that order.

Stepping from the train into the crowd, Roman heard, "Roman, my boy, I'm over here." Looking around, Roman spotted their chef, Vicente Domansky, waving at him and grinning broadly. They greeted each other warmly before heading home to the onslaught of family greetings. Roman immediately asked, "What special food do you have for me?

Domansky laughed and responded with his usual, "You will just have to wait and see. Let's be off. The family is waiting."

Roman was pensive. This would probably be the last Easter spent with his family for a long time. Graduation from the academy was only about two months away since the officer's training had been shortened from four years to two years due to the Great War.

Roman's dream of becoming a naval officer was becoming a reality which occupied most of his thoughts. He wondered, *how will father react to me when he sees me in naval uniform?*

Roman's mother often wrote and, of course, wanted to know where he would be sent. His response to his mother's question was, "I don't know where I will be sent after graduation. All I know is that it will be aboard a ship somewhere." He really didn't care. He was just excited.

Easter was a national celebration and a very special time throughout Russia with the Orthodox religious atmosphere setting the scene for the day. Each Easter Eve, bells would ring out from the Tower of Ivan the Great in Moscow reflecting the joy of everyone. It was a time of family reunions, parties and dances. Masses, special foods and singing in the streets added to the festivities.

The Sturmer family always enjoyed the Orthodox Easter tradition of colored eggs: the *"pisanki"*, richly ornamented eggs in two, three, or four colors; and the *"krashenki"*, one-color, unornamented eggs. People presented eggs of either kind to one another. Even in Czar Nicholas Romanoff's house, colored eggs were presented to the Russian nobility.

Roman visualized which of the foods he desired to eat first. It was no secret, he loved to eat. He especially liked special treats such as *"kulich" and "paskha"* which were carried to church and set out on long tables to be blessed by the priest. Nuts (usually almonds) and candied or dried fruit were also favorites. The priest would often accommodate his wealthier parishioners by making a special call to bless their food at their home.

The *paskha* mixture was placed in a mold—often like a four-sided pyramid-- which had been lined with a fine cheesecloth wrung out of cold water. It was then decorated with nuts or candy or spread on a slice of kulich.

Preparation of the classic *kulich* was time consuming. It was filled with candied fruit, almonds and raisins and always baked in a special kind of pan—usually tall and cylindrical, somewhat like a coffee can. The bread, or cake, when done, was decorated with white frosting drizzled down the sides. Along the sides, spelled out in pieces of candied fruit, were the letters XB, representing the Cyrillic letters for *"Christos voskres"*, "Christ is risen"

***

Despite the war between Germany and the Central Powers, Easter was still being celebrated. The war was dragging on, or more precisely,

36

stagnating. Russia was repeatedly stalled somewhere, and in desperate need of aid from its allies, France and Britain. Trains blocked other trains; trucks blocked traffic in the larger cities; and people blocked and pushed one another in crowded railroad stations. It seemed everyone was for themselves.

Closer to the front, troops and equipment were bogged down in frozen mud or quagmires, depending on the season. Everywhere—in cities and towns—people stood in long lines hoping to get some food. Distribution issues and crop failures increased the problem. At this point the more affluent hadn't felt the deprivation as strongly as the more impoverished.

Because of the shortened school term, due to the war, Roman's final studies were upon him and he hoped he could study without interruptions, although he had his doubts.

Kira, Roman's sister, was studying at the same college with a young woman named Xenia Harvey who wanted to have a party and celebrate during Pancake Week, *Maslenitsa*. This was the festive time before the Russian Orthodox Church Easter observances began and a time of restricting what was eaten.

When Xenia went to the Sturmer household to deliver Kira an invitation for the pre-Lenten party, Xenia's eyes lit up when she saw Roman for the first time; the young cadet home on leave from the naval academy. "H-m-m-m," she thought then offered him an invitation, "You are also invited to my party." At this time, Roman was nearly six feet tall, but was down to a heavy, but trim, 200 pounds from his previous 300 pounds due to the rigorous training required of the cadets. Xenia found him quite a dashing figure.

Roman protested that he didn't want to go, but Kira had her way. Roman escorted her. "When the day of the party came," he later told a classmate, "my sister insisted that I escort her. I agreed on the condition that I would not stay at the party, but would go back home and somebody else would escort her back home. I wasn't much for partying. I preferred to stay home and rest from our hard studies."

When he and Kira reached Xenia's home, the door opened and a bunch of young people would not let him go. So he stayed and rather enjoyed the evening. They danced, played games such as *spin-the-bottle* and had refreshments. Xenia's brothers and some other friends were also there at the party so it was much larger than she originally expected, but she was delighted. The studious Roman quickly became addicted to the games and dances and loved the challenges—to his surprise. He didn't pay a particle of attention to the hostess, Xenia. He danced with another girl named Margie and paid more attention to her. He tried to dismiss the evening as not being impressed with anything at all.

Xenia, whose large mischievous eyes kept darting looks at Roman was clearly attracted to him, although Roman paid no attention to her. She particularly enjoyed the game in which people wrote funny things to share with the others. But, far more pleasing to her was that Roman found out "little Margie" wasn't very bright—even if she *was* pretty.

Ostensibly unimpressed, Roman, however, was not through with the party. In a few days, Kira told Roman, with a twinkle in her eyes, "You should write a letter to Xenia to thank her for the party." Reluctantly, he wrote the letter, but in French, with his sister's help. She secretly thought it was very funny. Surprisingly, this started the correspondence. Roman tried to recall if it was even at the party when he'd met her the first time. He couldn't remember. But Xenia remembered!

Roman had another surprise: this correspondence would become an habitual thing between them. *She* claimed to Kira that she knew intuitively that it would be ongoing. "I found his writing to me in French rather humorous at first."

Xenia continued writing to him and he wrote back. It even continued when Roman returned to the Academy in St. Petersburg. Roman wrote in French. She thought it strange that he started in French because she wasn't even French. Her mother laughed all the time, thinking that perhaps it was as some historical accounts claim; French was considered a more desirable language. It was used greatly in the more aristocratic community because the Russian language itself sounded too coarse.

Roman was puzzled, not that they were writing in French, but that he was writing to Xenia at all. His plans never even considered such an acquaintance. And he mused; *I don't even know her background!*

He usually didn't leave the ship to go ashore, so the only distractions he had from his studies and watches were reading and writing daily letters to Xenia. Almost always he had immediate replies from her. He thought mostly of his upcoming graduation.

The very cold weather was over. A slight chill turned to warmth and sun as graduation day from the naval academy in St Petersburg arrived. It was a time of celebration for the graduates. All the cadets were in their dress uniform. Roman was pleased that all his family attended, even his father. Later in the day, he stood proudly in position on the *Aurora* for viewing time. When Xenia came on board, he tried to keep a look of surprise and pleasure off his face. After all, he was on duty. It surprised him even more to notice how pretty she looked. He really hadn't given her much thought until then, despite the letters. Kira caught Roman's look. Slyly she gave Roman a smug look.

Before the day was over, he showed the family his room. With a little smile, his mother bent to Roman and said, "This looks more comfortable than the couch. No wonder you liked it here." Roman responded with a smile.

Chapter 6

Through the almost daily exchange of letters Roman learned some of Xenia's childhood prior to the party.

Although she was living in Moscow now, Xenia Nicholas Harvey was born on a typically cold and windy winter St. Petersburg day, October 27, 1898, with temperatures at freezing point. She was the first-born of Nicholas J. Harvey and his wife, Nadejhda M. Dobriansky, a Russian noblewoman.

Nicholas Harvey, a British subject living in Russia and editor of an English newspaper, had been partially educated in Russia but retained British citizenship his entire life. Xenia and her six siblings—four boys and two girls—were British subjects.

Xenia wrote, "When I was nine, father moved us 400 miles from St. Petersburg to Moscow to start a newspaper. He is analytical and a progressive thinker. He felt it was time to make that move considering that industrialization and urbanization were on the upward-bound." Railroads now radiated out from Moscow and the many much-used waterways, like the Moskva River, flowed through the busy, bustling city. The area was host to intense social activity and artistic endeavors which Harvey felt was good for the family—especially his wife--as well as a newspaper.

Moscow was a city of many green trees and parks. When one looked down upon the city, one could enjoy a magnificent view of the gilded spires and the painted domes of numerous ornate cathedrals and churches. Monasteries with their gray walls stood in grim, stark contrast to the surrounding beauty.

Xenia was proud of her heritage and loved sharing it with Roman. The family had first lived in a big house on the outskirts of Moscow.

41

Her mother, having grown up on the family estate in the Voronezh region, had been quite the independent woman before marriage and remained very social and industrious all during the children's childhood.

"We also have some German heritage like you," Xenia wrote to Roman. "Father lived for a time in the Volga region. My grandmother, Anastasia Schmidt may have been raised in one of the numerous, small German colonies along the banks of the beautiful and busy Volga river. I know that one of the first flour millers of that region was named Schmidt and there's a possible connection to our family, but I'm not sure."

The family moved to a big apartment in town in 1910 when Xenia was 12-years-old. She told Roman, "I welcomed the move because I like to be active and here I have more opportunities to express myself. We all went to school like other children, but we had governesses who taught us French and German. Our nanny cared for us while mother flitted about doing her charity work and visiting friends."

"Our family has a rule that we eat dinner together. Father has always made very good money—about $10,000 a year—I think, so we eat well. I've never liked the borscht, but I have to be careful about complaining. The rule is that we have to eat everything we're served; children are supposed to be seen but not heard."

Xenia's family enjoyed frequent outings together. They would go to the many churches, museums, and magnificent buildings with all their displayed collections of jewels, paintings, and other art for which Russia was known. The family especially liked to walk through the numerous beautiful gardens and public parks: magnificent statues were a part of Moscow's heritage and available for everyone to see. The richness of Moscow's architecture was world-renowned, especially Saint Basil's Cathedral with its elegant colorful onion domes typical of Russian Orthodox churches. From these excursions the children developed an appreciation for all forms of art.

School finished at three-thirty in the afternoon. The children promptly went home and prepared for dinner at five. But first, they were required to practice their music. Mrs. Harvey was an accomplished pianist and tried to teach the children to play, but she was so nervous that the teaching was unsuccessful. Only two of the brothers liked it. Xenia informed Roman that, for her, each day was a ritual. "I hated the lessons. My heart wasn't in it. After dinner it was time for homework which was very difficult. However, my routine didn't include time for me to learn to cook or sew. I was happy about that!"

Xenia was called "Keeper of the Cupboard". The apartment's kitchen and walk-in cupboards were very large and whenever her parents weren't around, they trusted her with the keys to the locked cupboards. When the other children pestered her for sweets or other goodies, she would tell them a firm "No", but eventually relented. She thought them rascals and couldn't remain firm.

The war broke out before Xenia was allowed to go to social balls, but she had many friends. At that time, she was in what would correspond to the second year in high school in the United States.

Xenia continued to Roman, "Serving the less fortunate was expected of us, so I was very anxious to help with the war effort as it escalated. When I pleaded with Mother for permission to help, she talked the family doctor into allowing me to help in a private hospital."

However, one day when she was 15, she was cleaning in a room in which an injured soldier was undergoing surgery. One of the nurses fainted, so the doctor turned to an interested Xenia, and asked, "How about you helping?"

It turned out that Xenia was a natural at nursing. The doctor preferred her to some of the other nurses, so it became her occupation after school hours. She was escorted with her governess there and when she was finished, the governess came and took her home.

"All the doctors smiled and laughed at me, remarking, 'You are so young,'" she wrote Roman.

Like so many upper-class Russian women were doing, Mrs. Harvey felt it her duty to contribute to the war effort. Besides, she also liked to escape from her daily routine. With some of her friends, she knitted scarves and sweaters, went to meetings, and held raffles and exhibitions to raise money. There were numerous charity efforts.

Xenia's family sent parcels and gifts to the front at Christmas and Easter, and other special occasions. Since the brothers were too young to pay much attention to what was occurring, they weren't involved in any war effort. Her youngest brother was only one-year-old at the time.

Xenia's father worked long hours at his newspaper, *Otro Russii (Russia's Morning)*. In essence, it belonged to a trust of big millionaire industrialists. The government, which was becoming more restrictive, considered the newspaper too liberal. However, the industrialists invested much money in the paper and often put in articles and controversial items concerning the government. In the event an article appeared which the government thought was *too* liberal, the paper was required to pay a fine. Sometimes the fines were paid; other times the trust chose not to pay them.

On one such occasion, in 1913, when Xenia was 15, the trust chose not to pay the fine for an offense—so a man on her father's payroll went to "jail" in place of her father. Mr. Harvey's "substitute" was married to a very rich lady who was said to love her husband, but she was "so tired" that she didn't bother to pay the fine for him, and consequently, he stayed in confinement. In any case, he didn't suffer too harshly. Since he was a "replacement" for Xenia's father, he was privileged to receive his food from a restaurant. He even had a special room where his wife could visit him. In essence, it was more like detention rather than prison. This was common practice at that time. Harvey foresaw more difficult times coming and observed that many others were oblivious to what was happening to their country. He desired to make them more aware of what was happening.

In writing to Roman about more of her teenage years, Xenia explained: "I was sixteen when I graduated from school. I had finished courses and wanted to be an army nurse. Then, I planned to go to the front and work. During that last summer, we went to my grandmother's estate in Voronezh and stayed there while I worked. Every morning I got up at 5 o'clock and walked five miles—probably about four miles—to a camp."

"The hospital was not a big one, nor very elaborate. It was more like a camp where they treated soldiers and officers. They laughed at me because of my age, but I knew I was a good worker."

It was at that hospital that Xenia decided to study medicine to become a doctor. But at seventeen, she was too young to go to medical school. Usually, a medical student had to be at least nineteen years old. Xenia's interest in medicine may have been further intensified by the knowledge that she had a very notable ancestor, Dr. William Harvey, who in the 1600's was credited with discovering how the blood circulates in the human body.

Diminutive and lively, Xenia had a talent for dancing and enjoyed taking lessons while she was still in school in Moscow. In another letter to Roman, she wrote "We had a very good school and an excellent teacher from the famous Bolshoi Theatre. He was a perfectionist, about 50 years old. We all thought him to be a very old man. He thought I was good so he gave me the lead in little productions we performed during the Christmas season. I asked if I could take private lessons and my mother agreed, but cautioned, 'Don't tell Papa because he might think you want to be an actress'!"

"I didn't want to be an actress. I want to be a doctor," she wrote. Little did she know, but those dancing lessons would later prove to be of great benefit.

Because Xenia's father had some influence in St Petersburg, and because of her British papers, Xenia was finally admitted to the St Petersburg Women's Medical Institute to pursue her dream. She would start her studies in the fall.

After the Revolution broke out in earnest, there were fewer social events to attend. There were many restrictions, but Xenia managed to go several times to the naval academy in St. Petersburg to visit cousins. Even after she met Kira Sturmer in her last year of school in Moscow, their social life had been curtailed.

Little did they realize how fiercely their canopy of youthful protection would be shattered.

Xenia Harvey
(unknown period of time)

Chapter 7

Roman could not have wished for a grander, more honorable assignment than the one he received at graduation in the summer of 1916. Newly commissioned Lieutenant Sturmer was appointed an officer aboard the *Empress Maria*, one of 35 officers and 1200 crewmen who manned the dreadnought-class warship.

Excitement was evident in the letters he wrote to Xenia. He was living his dream and he treated all the details of his ship as if the ship was a person! Xenia learned more about ships than she ever wanted to know.

"The *Maria* is a 23,000-ton battleship—much faster and with a lower profile than our earlier battleships, and more heavily armed and armored. She has a speed of 21 knots, although she's already achieved up to 24 knots. She carries 12 twelve-inch guns in four electrically operated turrets plus 20 five-inch guns, and her armor plate is a foot thick around its turrets and other areas which need extra protection. She is the pride of the Black Sea fleet and she's my ship."

***

The primary purpose of the Black Sea fleet was to blockade the Bosporus against any enemy infiltration from the Mediterranean. It was also an attempt to blockade the Turkish coal-producing region of Zonguldak along the Black Sea's southeast coast in order to prevent the Turks from getting coal to the Germans. Considerable activity had occurred here since the start of the Great War. Since early 1916, Russia had made ten voyages to the Anatolian coast to plant mines on the approaches to the Bosporus. As a result, 14 Turkish steamships and over 50 sailing vessels were sunk.

Roman arrived at the *Empress Maria's* berth in her base port of Sevastopol late one summer afternoon several weeks after graduation. He stepped proudly onto the deck according to Russian protocol for officers arriving aboard ship with his hat under his arm. The deck officer ordered a sailor to lead Roman to the *Maria's* executive officer, Commander Gorodysky. "A real man," Roman murmured to himself as he faced the heavily built officer. Cordial but formal, Gorodysky in turn directed him to a cabin amid-ship where he could change his uniform for dinner. "We meet at seventeen hundred out on the after deck," he said.

Map from Wikipedia

Roman saw it was a very small cabin. It had no port hole, only a vent in the ceiling which led out onto the deck. It was an odd-shaped cabin. The end abutted one wall of the aft command post, which could be used if the forward command post under the bridge was destroyed. The cabin was oblong, wider at one end, with the upper and lower bunk against one wall. A small desk stood beside the doorway, which pleased Roman.

In writing Xenia, he told her, "My room isn't what I hoped it to be. And, I don't like my cabin mate, either."

His cabin mate was a former Academy classmate who wasn't good for much but drinking. Flamboyant, he was a man who had little regard for naval regulations. With his habitual drinking in mind, Roman asked him to take the lower berth and he would take the upper. "I don't want to be in the path of any sickness you might encounter after a drinking bout. I don't want to be a victim of one of your 'waterfalls'."

After inspecting his cabin and his new roommate, Roman was taken to the outdoor dining area—two tables on the after deck under an awning stretched from a guard rail on one side of the ship and then across three guns of a turret to the opposite railing. He was directed to a long table with 12 officers already seated and presided over by a senior lieutenant. Roman introduced himself and in turn was welcomed by the other officers. More officers were seated at another table on the other side of the deck.

Stewards delivered dinner on large platters, and the officers passed them around. One platter was filled with long, yellow knobby vegetables that Roman had never seen before. He lifted one to his plate trying not to look puzzled, but he wasn't sure what to do with it. He took his knife and fork and tried to cut it, but he succeeded only in making the strange looking thing skid off his plate. Retrieving it, he felt foolish—especially when he looked up to find the other officers laughing. Among them was a close friend from the Academy, Vladimir Fock, who was called Volodya. He rescued Roman by explaining the skittish vegetable was corn-on-the cob and showed him how to eat it. Roman was made to pay for his clumsiness. Good-naturedly, he asked, "Okay. What's the fine?" He had to buy a bottle of wine for his table.

In the conversation around the table, Roman learned how he'd come to be assigned to the *Empress Maria*. The ship's officers received a list of Academy grads and made a choice of whom they wanted. Roman recognized one of the officers at the table as having presided over their mess table at the Academy. He'd graduated the year before and remembered Sturmer as a serious student and the head of his class in his studies. Roman learned that it was his recommendation that had confirmed Roman as the choice for the *Maria*.

As if the corn-on-the-cob incident hadn't been an embarrassing enough initiation, Roman had an even more humiliating experience later the same evening. He drew deck duty on his first night aboard, from 8 p.m. to midnight. Admiral Kolchak, the distinguished naval commander, was on the bridge during Roman's watch. The proximity of this famous Russian patriot scared him to death. It tied Roman's stomach in knots so that he took extra care to keep a close watch on anything and everything that came close to the ship. Things went fine. Then, he saw the phosphorescent trail of something heading straight for the ship.

"Torpedo!" he called out at the top of his lungs.

A sailor near him calmly corrected his vision. "It's all right, sir. It's just a dolphin. They're all over the waters here."

Roman nodded dumbly, mumbled some incoherent thanks, and moved away trying to hide his stupidity in the comfort of the shadows.

* * *

Lieutenant Sturmer's entrance into World War I took place at the fringe of the main conflict which was centered in France and Germany. Russia was an undependable ally for a host of reasons. It was totally unprepared to fight. Its military presence was a makeshift thing with poorly trained armies stifled by lack of weapons, ammunition, clothing, and all the other supplies necessary to support a military operation. In addition to all of this weakness, Russia struggled to move what pitiful supplies they did have over incredibly long distances to its army's front lines. This diminished Russia's unorganized efforts even more. The crowning agony for all of Russia, though, was the turmoil in which its government was embroiled. The czarist government was in chaos: Czar Nicholas' lack of leadership, strategy, and determination along with the growing radical political upheaval was made worse by the ominous Bolshevik presence—an increasing threat of wildness and violence.

The Black Sea was a long way physically from the rest of the Great War, but Turkey's decision to ally itself with Germany brought everything closer. The Allies were trying to fight their way through the Dardanelles to get to the Bosporus, the entrance from the

Mediterranean to the Black Sea the southern entrance to Russia. The significant target of both the Allies, Britain and France, and the Central Powers Germany and Austria was Istanbul. Istanbul, formerly Constantinople, the center of Eastern Christianity, a kind of eternal city, had been ruled over the centuries by numerous nations as the tides of wars had ebbed and flowed. Turkey still considered itself the great city's guardian. With Germany as a partner, Turkey could make sure no Allied army would force its way into the Black Sea.

Turkey had no navy to speak of. The two warships it did have, the *Goeben* and the *Breslau,* gifts from Germany, became the targets of Russia's Black Sea Fleet, the *Empress Maria* and her sister ship the *Empress Catherine the Great.* A third ship, the *Alexander III,* still under construction, would help Russia control the Black Sea. The *Goeben's* ability to cruise at 27 knots, was faster than Russia's dreadnoughts' 21 knot speed, but she was smaller at 22,300 tons, and carried only ten 11-inch guns and twelve 6-inch guns. The *Breslau* was merely a light cruiser, displacing only 4,550 tons and carrying only twelve 4-inch guns. In addition, the *Maria* and the *Catherine the Great* also carried heavier armor, with protection on its belts and turrets reaching a maximum of 12 inches thick. Also, their guns were given an especially high angle of elevation, allowing them to fire at a distance of about 25 miles, a greater distance than any other dreadnought at sea.

These four active ships were the major combatants in the Black Sea. Many smaller craft were engaged one way or another, but these four prowled the Black Sea day and night searching for each other, sometimes coming within range. The German and Russian ships evaded and dodged each other, game-like, though always with lethal intent.

***

"I was named officer in charge of the *Maria's* Gun Turret No.4," Roman wrote Xenia. "On this, my first tour of the ship, I admit to being enchanted; yes, enchanted, with all I see and am doing...but I miss seeing you." A great part of him had not grown up from the nine-year-old boy who was mesmerized those years before in Gdansk. "Of the 35 officers and 1,200 crewmen, I am in charge of 70 men in my Turret No. 4 crew."

Roman quickly excelled in all his responsibilities by learning all there was to know about the sophisticated equipment. It was all electric, nearly foolproof. Shells and powder were brought up from ammunition magazines below decks by hydraulic hoists. Preparation for firing each shell was precise: one shell, two cartridges, a silk bag of gunpowder, an ignition cap. Then the breach would close and the gun could fire. But not before.

When the *Empress Maria* would fire its big guns, the first salvo would be from turrets 1 and 3; the second, from 2 and 4. There would be 10 seconds between salvos. In that interim, the chief gunnery officer would watch the first salvo's strike and call to turrets, "Turrets 2 and 4, less two and less two, or plus two" or whatever, depending on whether the first salvo was long or short of its target. Then the crew would calculate in between those two in order to get right on target, and by the third or fourth salvo, they would nearly always score a direct hit.

Roman's store of gunnery knowledge came in large measure from an old-timer, a non-commissioned officer named Shapovaloff. This stocky seaman took a liking to Sturmer because he asked the old-timer to "Tell me everything because I know nothing."

There was always something for Roman's curiosity to explore. He spent much of his off duty time visiting all the parts of the *Empress Maria*. Everything about the ship fascinated him. He was particularly amazed at the cleanliness of the engine room, unlike the engine rooms on other ships he had seen during training: Roman had found them notoriously dirty, oily, smelly: It had been grueling duty. Nothing like this had ever been in any text book at Academy. The *Maria's* engine room shone like an officers' wardroom in Roman's mind.

As an officer, Roman also had time to help the ship's chaplain, an old white-bearded priest who wore a little round, narrow-upturned-brimmed hat and a white tunic that matched his beard. Roman helped teach and encourage about 25 sailors who could only read and write very slowly. This volunteer duty was a natural for Roman, who already had knowledge of a half dozen languages and enjoyed helping others.

***

Sturmer's superior officer was Lt. Comdr. Engelman Urieff, assistant to the executive officer of the *Maria*. Under his command, the *Empress Maria's* main duty was always to track the *Goeben* and the *Breslau*. She also escorted smaller vessels in forays against Bulgaria and Turkish ports, helped bombard those two ports and generally attempted to keep the two Turkish/German ships at bay. They were faster and were forever eluding the *Empress Maria*.

Thanks to his earnestness with Shapovaloff in assuming command of Turret No. 4, Roman came to the attention of one of the ship's navigating officers, Lt. Grivtzoff, who persuaded him to take a post-graduate class in navigation. Grivtzoff, a married man with two sons, also liked Roman for the same reason Shapovaloff did. He was responsible, attentive and eager to learn. Roman valued his advice and after a few months of off-duty study aboard ship, he became a graduate navigating officer—No. 1 in his class. He was now eligible to serve as a navigator anywhere. That would hold him in good stead in the future.

But, before these new navigating skills could be put to use, Roman's career took an abrupt and tragic change of direction.

J & P Oliver

Chapter 8

The early morning chill still clung to the breezes coming off the Black Sea. It was not surprising as October always heralded oncoming winter, even here in Russia's warmer southern climate. The *Empress Maria* had come in last night from another fruitless search for Turkey's *Goeben* and the *Breslau* and now rested dockside next to one of the piers jutting into Sevastopol's harbor.

A mist hanging low over the area muffled the voices of a few locals in the area. As the war situation grew more rampant, few citizens were about unless absolutely necessary. Most stayed away from the docks. Already the morning crews were busy unloading ammunition from the turret magazines onto the shore stores in preparation for the next hunt. The crew always took care and handled the ammunition according to strict regulations. The procedure never varied.

Roman was still asleep at 6:30 a.m., October 7, 1916, when he was jolted from his bunk with such force that he felt the *Empress Maria* had been hit. Shouts of "a Zeppelin has attacked us!" came from the passageway outside his cabin, confirming his fear.

As he later told a superior officer, "I jumped up and couldn't find my shoes or pants because my orderly had taken them to clean. I found other shoes and pants, put on a greatcoat and cap, and ran on deck."

"The sight which greeted me was horrible. A pillar of smoke from the forward section of the ship rose two to three hundred feet in the air. Flames almost as high shot up, and some of the crew ran past me, burned badly. I went forward and helped some of the poor fellows, dragging them to a safer area at the stern area of the deck."

"There was a terrible explosion, then another...and another."

Thirty-five powder magazines had blown.

When at sea, some shells and powder charges, in silk sacks five inches in diameter and about three feet long and each weighing about 30 pounds, were customarily kept on deck at the ready in a ship's gun turrets. When shore-bound, all ammunition was transferred back to the below-deck magazines. After only three such transfers from magazine to turret to magazine, gun crews had orders to dispose of the powder sacks ashore and bring aboard new supplies. The change of temperature between powder magazines and turrets had a deteriorating effect on the powder, making it unstable and unreliable. It could explode at any time, or not explode at all inside one of the guns.

A tired and sluggish crew was now making a transfer for disposal on this morning of October 7, 1916. "Move along. We haven't got all day!" they were ordered. With that order, a sailor tried to hurry and accidently dropped one of the ammo sacks.

Fire erupted instantly. The forward 10 five-inch guns blew up carrying the No. One 12-inch gun turret into the air and dropping it, tilted, back on deck, listing heavily to starboard.

Sailors staggered and ran screaming, "What is happening? What do we do?" They were frantic and didn't know what to do. It was immediately clear in Roman's mind that this was total disaster and he knew the impact would remain there for years. The ship's command post, protected by 12-inch-thick steel, along with the foremast and the forward smokestack, shuddered upward and all fell overboard. Then with a kind of inexorable regularity, the other magazines exploded in flame and smoke on both sides of the ship from bow to stern.

Admiral Alexander Kolchak, Commander-in-Chief of the Black Sea fleet, came aboard for a brief time. "Open the sea valves! Open the valves!" He hoped the inrushing water would douse the explosions.

Roman parroted the order but doubted its effectiveness. *It seems a good plan good in theory. But the bulkheads are badly shaken by the constant explosions. The water's already running along the full length of the ship. I don't see how it can work.*

Matters grew worse. Debris and fumes added to the now smoke-filled air diminishing remaining visibility.

As Roman helped the wounded, he heard the captain shout, "Abandon ship!" The *Empress Maria* listed first to port, then to starboard, then with an agonizing gasp, capsized."

The *Empress Maria's* higher-ranking officers used the ladder over the port side. Peering over, Roman saw small craft taking them aboard and to safety. He was just about to step onto one of the rungs of the ladder when another officer, a good friend of his, blocked him.

"I am an officer senior to you," the officer said. "You must let me go first." Roman dutifully stepped aside.

The officer crowding in was the last to use the ladder. The ship began listing faster and faster to port; the ladder was now hanging clear of the hull, far out from the port side of the ship and out of Roman's grasp. Escape that way was now out of the question.

Roman ran to the starboard side and climbed over the railing. "Oh, God, I'm scared. Help me!" he voiced repeatedly as he attempted to walk along the side of the hull as it came up out of the water. He stumbled against the anti-submarine and anti-torpedo netting along the whole side of the ship and fell. As he slipped down the side, the clawing barnacles shredded his overcoat. The keel stopped his plunge momentarily before he tumbled into the water.

In terrible turbulence caused by the capsizing ship, Roman was sucked down to the very bottom of the harbor. He started to swallow water and thought it was the end for him. His thoughts were of his family—and Xenia. He surfaced again seconds later when the rolling current began its upward thrust, but he had no control. In those moments he tried to remember all the swimming lessons he'd in the Academy, but it was useless. He was tossed about like a little piece of wood before he struck his head on something and lost consciousness.

In one short hour Russia's prize battleship had sunk, not in a fierce battle, but from self-inflicted wounds right in the harbor.

***

The first thought Roman had as he struggled back to consciousness was that the world was upside down. He found himself in one of the small rescue craft scurrying around the *Empress Maria* carrying dead bodies and injured seamen to the pier. As he regained consciousness, he realized he was draped over a hawser hitch, head down, as if to drain like a drying tarpaulin. Groggy and in pain from tumbling down the ship's hull on his back and legs, clawed raw by barnacles, he was barely aware of being taken to a smaller ship, the *Eustacius*, and placed in a cabin with only his pants, tunic, and overcoat.

A ship's medic came in and with the help of another crewman they removed Roman's wet clothes. Then they cleaned and tended to his injuries. As he lay still, gradually warming up under new dry blankets, he slowly became more aware of his surroundings. The dizziness and nausea began to lessen—but not the sense of loss as he started to recall everything.

The cabin Roman was placed in belonged to a good friend of his, Ladislaus Charnetsky. Coming in from outside and standing over him, Charnetsky smiled down as he saw Sturmer's eyes open, and placed a rough hand on his shoulder. He disappeared for a moment and came back with a glass of wine, handing it to Roman without a word. A nod and a half smile expressed his relief that his friend was alive.

"Don't move," he finally spoke. "I will be back shortly." He returned in a few minutes with a new uniform. "I hope this fits you, my friend."

Roman lay there for a long while shivering without attempting to try on the new clothes. He could barely raise his head enough to sip the wine from time to time. Gradually the shivering stopped and he felt his strength returning. But he never did hear the order for all of the *Empress Maria's* crew to assemble aboard another cruiser, her sister ship, the *Empress Catherine the Great*.

Roman was the only survivor still aboard the *Eustacius*, and when he was spotted, he was taken immediately to join the rest of the crew. It was a shock for everyone to see him still alive. Many had seen him plunge down the side of the *Empress Maria* and be tossed into the debris-filled churning water. Even his immediate superior officer, Lt. Urieff, whom Roman had always considered very strict, embraced him emotionally, crying and telling him how glad he was that Roman was alive.

Once aboard the cruiser, Lieutenant Sturmer and the other grim-faced, surviving officers began restoring some kind of order. Despite his condition, Roman was placed in charge of the burial detail. In the days that followed, this grueling, unpleasant task became even more difficult because of the cold weather

Bodies, bodies, and more bodies. Parts of bodies. So many. The stench of death now permeated everything. It was fruitless to even try and ignore it. More than once Roman felt that it was the will of God that he was alive. It must be so, since they estimated that more than five hundred fellow crewmen and officers of the *Empress Maria* had died in the catastrophe. Gradually, investigating officers pieced together what had caused the tragedy and verified that a crewman had accidentally dropped a bag of gunpowder which had caught fire and set off the great holocaust.

Crewmen hastily hammered caskets together to hurry along the grim burial task, and large common graves were dug in the local cemetery. In charge of the honor detail, Sturmer and his men haul wagon loads of 50 bodies—both complete and incomplete—in caskets to the graveyard at the edge of Sevastopol. There, in a simple ceremony they gave an honor salute for each victim, firing three shots for each man; fifty caskets were placed in each common grave and covered. Later a monument was erected over the whole plot in their memory.

As the days passed, Roman recuperated—physically, at least. Other aspects of his aftermath continued over a much longer time. The memories were gruesome and continued to penetrate his thoughts. He kept thinking about the burial of so many of his friends. And, he'd lost all his possessions, including his special little treasure box of rubles "stolen" years ago from his special grandfather, *Deduskha* Kazimir. Gone, all of it, at the bottom of the sea. At first, the loss was painful, childlike in intensity, even disorienting. But, that feeling gradually weakened, leaving a scar that he sensed would never quite disappear. All desire for personal belongings was gone. He determined to never again allow possessions to hold any great meaning for him.

More than once Roman would stand on the pier by himself and look out at the upturned hulk of the *Empress Maria* protruding starkly from the water. The only sign of where his box of treasures lay was a small stream of water spouting from some crack in the hull, a watery gravestone marking childhood memories.

Chapter 9

Xenia was excited: She felt like an adult pursuing her own dream at last. In the early fall of 1916, she went to live with an aunt in Petrograd and attended the Women's Medical Institute while her family continued living in Moscow. She was so occupied with school that she was unaware of the tragedy that had befallen the Black Sea fleet. She wondered why she hadn't heard from Roman. Therefore, she had no idea of his close escape from death in the sinking of the *Empress Maria* in October.

St. Petersburg's name was changed in 1914 to Petrograd for political reasons. Some thought St. Petersburg sounded too German.

Later the school's name was again changed to Pavlov State Medical University of Saint-Petersburg.

The Petrograd Women's Medical Institute was an exceptional school. It was founded in 1897 and reputed to be the first Russian higher medical school especially for women.

Xenia was an apt and committed student. One day, when working on a cadaver in a morgue, an instructor told her that her mother's father, Mitrophan S. Dobriansky, had wanted to be a doctor but he couldn't stand working on the cadavers and had fainted. This created some concern about Xenia's ability—especially from her mother—but Xenia told the instructor, "I am very cold-blooded and capable. I also work about two hours a day at the naval academy. So I will be just fine."

By December, a series of events disrupted Russia's traditional way of life—perhaps forever. More and more people became fearful that the political situation was no longer a temporary uprising. It started with the killing of the man people called the "mad monk", Rasputin, in December 19th by poisoning him and then throwing him into the river.

Xenia had disagreed with her mother one day about the situation before she left for school. Her mother insisted that she pay more attention to political matters. However, Xenia just passed off her mother's concern saying to her, "You know how it is with us young people." She confessed, "We hear but we don't pay much attention. We have our own ideas and opinions. We think you older people don't know everything." She thought to herself, *It's all trash and I'll do better — I know myself—what I'll do when I get married and my life will be wonderful. I'll be a real person!*

However, Rasputin's murder forced Xenia to pay attention to what was going on, as it did everyone else. Neither she nor her family was ever completely taken in by the rumors that Rasputin and the royal families were intimates, although many believed it to be true. Actually, Rasputin was a peasant; a wandering "holy man" and womanizer with no name, like many peasants. The nickname "Rasputin" supposedly meant "dissolute". There were rumors that he had the gift of healing and the Czarina was apparently taken in and believed in his healing powers.

Xenia enjoyed being more social and still claimed she wasn't much into all the politics going on. She passed off Rasputin as just a hypnotist who rarely ever went to the Palace but often did his "healing" by telephone. "I think he's truly an evil man," she told her aunt, when he died in December of 1916. She continued, "There was much evil. I think they felt that by destroying that evil power they would liberate Russia. But, I think evil itself was really the start of all the tumult and forces against our government."

Many people chose to believe that the scandals and mediocrity that shook Russia in the succeeding months were simply the result of Rasputin's influence and scheming. However, 1916 was a time of many radicals. The secret police knew the danger was focused largely in the countryside. At first, they were aware of secret meetings and various leaders quietly traveling back and forth.

Xenia had never gone to the Palace because on the one occasion that her father went there, she was too young. He'd been summoned by the Prime Minister to the Czar who wanted her father to become a Russian citizen. Harvey declined and told Xenia. "I want to be on the safe side… That way I will be free to publish what I believe to be the truth."

The war itself was becoming a formidable enemy of Russia. The Central Powers, though stalemated along the Western Front, nevertheless were exerting more strength against Russia. Germany and Austria now posed an imminent threat at the western edge of the Black Sea. This threat was magnified by Russia's growing weakness; as a military power, she was simply unable to cope.

There were shortages of everything; food, ammunition and even things like kerosene for lamps. By now the railroads were in absolute confusion. Trains lined up without locomotives, and, even if engines were available, routes were clogged everywhere.

Peoples' faces reflected fear. Children's hands were tightly gripped by parents or nannies if they had to be outside.

Russian Revolution 1917 (Wikipedia)

Add to that, thousands of soldiers without rifles or ammunition deserted in ever increasing numbers: their will to fight thoroughly trampled. Police warned the Czar that the mood of the countryside had never been more dangerous. Yet, he was not overly concerned. The result was a growing national desire to stop the war, and the desire was turning to demand. In Petrograd, there was talk of a coup. More and more evident was the social and political unrest along with increased riots in Petrograd and Moscow.

As the months moved into 1917, the contrast—already sharp between the wealthy elite eating their fine foods and the poor standing in the long, cold lines waiting with their metal jugs hoping to get milk or bread—heightened dangerously. Nickolas Harvey was aware of the escalating problems, but tried to protect his family as much as possible from the terrible news.

In February, 1917, Xenia continued living in Petrograd with her aunt while she continued pursuing her studies at the medical school. Roman was still in the Black Sea area. Each was unaware of how the other was managing.

Winter's bitter cold weather enveloped everything in and around Petrograd. The River Neva was frozen over and the streets were dangerously icy. Everyone dressed in their warmest clothes. Twenty-two degrees Fahrenheit was the average *high* temperature. Unrest permeated the whole country. Food lines increased. People stood waiting in the icy weather and began hoarding portions of any food they managed to obtain by whatever means.

Heavy snowfall immobilized trains carrying grain. Extra troops were called up to keep the peace. The poor couldn't even afford wood for heating. Hardships drove people to desperate behavior, but the troops didn't stop radicals from inciting people to increasingly dangerous actions. Work stoppages grew more common inciting riots in many places. Grim, hungry faces were commonplace.

On Thursday, February 23rd, 1917, the International Woman's Day was held. The women of Petrograd were instrumental in agitating in an attempt to antagonize the men to revolt. Skilled workers joined strikers overturning trams to make a point, adding to the chaos. Friday, turned unusually mild and sunny. Angry shouts of "Down with the Monarchy!" were heard in the streets. Although there was little violence that day, factories closed as workers rallied together. Xenia's anxieties increased each day.

Then the killing began.

On Saturday, February 25th, Petrograd streetcars halted and work stoppage maximized, even at the banks. It was a day for the liberals and radical activists. They handed out leaflets and organized workers. Alexander Kerensky of the Duma government (an ineffective, elected semi-representative body) took an active role in denouncing the monarchy and fomenting confusion. More strangely, the Czar paid little attention to the problems in his own city.

By Sunday, the ice began to melt and a calm prevailed. Xenia enjoyed the spring-like day as she walked to church. She and others avoided police by walking on the still-frozen River Neva instead of crossing over the bridges of Petrograd.

A few days later, Xenia hastily grabbed a coat and school books and ran smiling down the steps to meet her friends. They laughed and exchanged ideas as they walked to the medical school thinking only of the present moment.

Peacefulness was short-lived and misleading. New chaos and increased danger followed. Suddenly, machine gun fire erupted. As it came closer and closer to them, they realized they were in extreme danger; terrified. "Don't run," Xenia screamed as they started to run away. "Fall down!" Terror had entered their lives without warning. Frantically, they fell to the street praying for their own safety. Xenia lay on the pavement until the gun fire ceased. When she dared to move her head, she saw death around her. People lay everywhere. Still. Death had also claimed several of her friends. *No...this can't be happening. I must get home... Will I make it? God, help me...*

Xenia did make it safely home that day. But, then came the revolutions that changed everything familiar to every Russian.

Czar Nicholas II's abdication on March 15th increased the turbulence and disunity throughout the country. It even affected the arts, always an important part of Russian society. In the long history of Russia, art had been largely controlled and purchased by the State and the court for additions to the Imperial collections.

Now Russian art—painting, music, literature, poetry, drama and dance—was also in the throes of a revolution, or focus, of its own. It started in the early 1900's. Wealthy patrons and society provided support and finance. Artisans vividly revealed the harsh reality of Russian life and awakened social consciousness in the extreme. Art flourished, once again. Both men and women started their own revolution in taste, style, and standards in the art world. Among the many sought-after treasures were the exquisite eggs created by the Fabergé family.

The early days of revolution, artisans had no time to generate great creativity regarding their own impressions. Individually, as well as a group, they actively pursued the preservation of cultural heritage rather than as individuals. Russia's ethnic and class tensions increased. Migrant towns and slums provided a backdrop for changes of modernity, opulent churches, and the nation's rising industrialization. Masses of people—including the uneducated—were influenced by the pictorial materials created by artists.

By April, when Xenia left school for Easter vacation, the turmoil had reached new levels. Fearing for her safety, her mother and father insisted she stay home—but her parents had no intention of leaving Russia, despite the increasing danger. British officials advised all British subjects to leave the country early in 1917 and offered to help. Nicholas Harvey refused to go. "No," he firmly told them, "I need to continue the paper."

To Xenia, her father stubbornly defended his decision, "I want to be on hand. I want to be in the country at the end. I am a newspaper man." He loved Russia and wanted his newspaper to be the first to announce the end of the revolution, and the end of communism. "Maybe, by and by, I'll send all of you out." Optimistically, he thought that the revolution would be over in three or four months.

Harvey was not a supporter of the Kerensky government: he found out early on that it was a fake; but he was a supporter of several friends in it and he wanted to do his part.

Xenia's mother didn't want to leave Russia because many of her relatives lived in Petrograd and other areas of Russia, so they ignored the warnings.

By the summer of 1917, Russia was in a fragile state of existence and conditions continued to deteriorate. The economy had basically failed. Peasants were on the rampage, physically taking over the land. Buildings were set afire and animals slaughtered. Rail lines were deliberately being cut and racial hatred was out-of-hand. Police protection against the mobs was non-existent. Few cabs and horse-drawn carriages were available. New money, rubles, come off presses with such speed that it was said that people had to cut the notes themselves with scissors. But, money had lost much of its power.

Reality was setting in and Harvey now feared for his family. He insisted they go to the country for a while but Xenia insisted on staying in Moscow. She wanted to work with her father at the paper. She was not one to be idle. Then came trouble: both she and her father were arrested as British subjects one summer day and put in prison along with other British and French subjects.

Xenia was terrified as they were transported to a prison outside Moscow. She recalled the death she'd seen, but she tried to be brave. She was somewhat relieved when she found the prison to be more like her idea of a concentration camp rather than some place where they would be killed. They were detained for three months then released and returned to Moscow.

In September, Sir George Buchanan, the British Ambassador shared with Harvey that he felt the Bolsheviks were so forceful that they could put down the government. Later that month, a rumor hit newspapers claiming that the Bolsheviks planned October 20th as the date to make an armed move. Gossip flourished and quickly spread. Newspapers revealed more details: dissension and chaos gripped the land. No one knew if the rumor was erroneous or not.

By late October, miserably cold and windy weather cut off telephone service adding new confusion. Newspapers were confiscated, especially right-wing papers: A new kind of terror intensified fears.

As tension increased, Lenin attempted to suppress all the presses—except for those of the Bolsheviks—and ordered censorship.

Persecutions were now occurring and escalating at a frightening rate. But the Harveys stayed—and suffered the violence.

Russia's strength had deteriorated greatly with the tragic loss of the *Empress Maria. Only two of our three dreadnought-class warships remain. My naval career has been turned upside down.*

In addition to Rasputin's murder, other daily disrupting events, had ushered in a whole new year of disaster.

Chapter 10

Roman and another survivor, his friend Volodya, were reunited aboard the *Empress Catherine the Great* and rejoiced at being assigned to the same cabin.

Volodya was a passionate young man with a perpetual sunny outlook. He contrasted well with Roman whose constant serious manner sometimes tended to dampen spirits. Not that Roman was morose; far from that. Roman had a healthy portion of his father's jolly manner, but he was simply more serious than the light-hearted Volodya. On many nights, Volodya, an exquisite pianist, had enchanted students at the Academy by his performances.

The roommates complemented one another, and they never grew tired of one another's company. This was a good thing, because though the *Empress Catherine's* cabin was larger than Roman's on the Empress Maria had been, the quarters were still cramped. Volodya stood well over six feet in height and was skinny as a rail. Whereas Roman, though nearly six feet tall himself, seemed dwarfed next to Volodya, although his own heavier girth made up for it.

The two men, so different, had much in common. Fock was considered a German name, as was Sturmer which meant "stormer", one who storms about. That didn't fit Roman, though, because he was far more sedate than stormy. For some Russians, their German names caused raised eyebrows. They shouldn't have, because many Germans had been invited to settle and farm along the Volga River many years prior. The war situation was making everyone suspicious.

Volodya's father was an officer in the Russian army, as was Roman's. His family also came from the same little farming area, Nizhny Novgorod on the Volga River, where Roman's ancestors had once lived. The soil was fertile and crops grew well. The rich abundant harvests provided food for much of Russia. Roman's father's father, a physician in Nizhny-Novgorod, had five sons and only one daughter. By Russian law one son from every family had to go into the military. So, Roman's father enlisted before he was drafted into the army. These similarities were factors in cementing Roman's and Volodya's friendship.

Roman became the commanding officer of the *Empress Catherine*'s 1st Company and also was assigned to command the forward starboard battery of five 130mm guns, an anti-destroyer and anti-submarine battery. It was here he felt he had finally met the Revolution. He felt like a naval officer, ready to fight for his country.

However, Roman was confronted daily with many memories as the overturned *Empress Maria's* quiet hull was nearby. A small fountain spouted up through a little hole marking the grave of Roman's childhood treasures.

In January, 1917, Roman was assigned to a small mine layer and sent to lay mines across the Bosporus Strait, one of many similar incidents aimed at bottling up the Constantinople harbor. Decorations were given for such duty, and in early February, while waiting for their recognition, they learned that a Turkish destroyer was blown up in that mine field. Roman received the award of the *Order of St. Anne, 4th class.* With the decoration came a saber with an inscription for courage during wartime.

However, the honor soon lost some of its glory, because the increasing revolutionary activity in Petrograd had flared violently into the open. As it turned out, it was a precursor to the far greater violence that would erupt months later, in November.

All through the winter and summer of 1917 the portents of the February fighting hung over the country. Russia was in such great upheaval that the Great War became secondary: Russia was unable to deal with itself, let alone Germany, Austria and Turkey and the rest of the Central Allies.

In mid-March, shocking word came that Czar Nicholas II had abdicated. This was the major advance notice of the collapsing government. It made all of the horrendous events—the futility of the Great War and the sinister, menacing Bolshevik presence—the world as Roman had always known it— frighteningly personal. For Roman, the Czar's departure had an immediate and tragic impact. Upon hearing the news, the executive officer of the *Empress Catherine* ordered the painting of the Czar hanging in the officers' wardroom be taken down.

"It was about midnight. I was in my bunk because I had to go on watch at four in the morning" Roman told investigating officers, "when Volodya rushed into the room, distraught, carrying the Czar's painting. He put it on the writing desk between our two bunks and stood staring at it. 'Now Russia will perish!' he cried and reached into a drawer. His hand came out holding a pistol, and he shot himself in front of my eyes, just a few feet from me. I knew what he was going to do and I leaped up to hit his hand, but I missed. He pulled the trigger and fell down dead."

The ship's doctor came, but there was nothing he could do. Volodya was dead and his body was taken ashore to the hospital.

"I was so shaken up I was trembling," Roman went on. "The doctor gave me something to drink and a friend took me to his cabin and wrapped blankets around me. I stayed there for several hours until I had to go on watch duties." He felt his own world was falling apart.

***

When more details of what had happened to the Czar trickled down to the ship, Roman realized something more: The revolution—long threatened—had actually begun. Discipline was shredding before his eyes. Volodya's death had somehow become a kind of signal—a signal as strong as the abdication of the Czar because it was closer and more personal. His impassioned act was a catalyst for some kind of mass action—as yet undefined—but as palpable as if it already was as solid as his death.

Later, making the rounds of inspecting the gun turrets, Roman sensed a change in the behavior of the crew. It was something he felt rather than saw. There was a difference in the atmosphere—a new tension—that required sharper attention. The crew seemed to be in a waiting mode, as if deciding something. The long stares of the crewmen in the dark night made everything very ominous to Roman, even though he could see nothing overt. At first he assumed the men were reacting to the news of the Czar, and also Volodya's suicide. Several small groups of crewmen huddled and talked together in hushed tones, watching Roman without any motion of greeting. This was so different from their usual habit of nodding or lifting a hand whenever they crossed paths. Where were their usual smiles and nods? And why are so many crewmen on deck at four in the morning? Something is afoot.

As he mulled this over, a voice at his elbow said, "Officer Sturmer? You are to report immediately to Captain Kuznetsky."

The voice disappeared into the night's shadows.

Captain Kuznetsky? What now? Roman asked himself.

This was not the time to ask questions: Roman hurried to report to the office.

"Pack your things," Captain Kuznetsky ordered Roman the moment he entered his office, "and get off this ship as fast as you can."

Roman stood still, shocked, momentarily speechless. He started to ask a question, but the captain shook his head and pointed to the door. "Go! Right now! There is a rumor rampant among the crew that Volodya was a German spy and blew up the Empress Maria! You were his roommate, his partner...a German spy, too!"

"What!" Roman, dumbfounded, managed to utter as he turned to leave. As he did, Captain Kuznetsky rose from behind his desk and came around to Roman. The captain's words added even more puzzlement to the entire night. He was a big man, taller and heavier than Roman, with a reputation for running excellent ships. Roman had heard of him many times back at the Academy and looked up to him.

The Captain spoke again in a quiet, almost gentle voice. "Sturmer, you know and I know that the rumor is not true, but we must act as if it is." He paused for a moment before going on, "Russia is in the hands of enemies now." He paused once again and said in fatherly tones, "You are a good officer, Sturmer. So, go! Immediately save yourself…and God Speed." Then he turned away briefly as if suddenly he was aware of how open he had been with Roman. Turning back, he had one more instruction, "Seaman Shopaloff will assist you in getting safely off the ship."

Chapter 11

Roman knew his life was in a precarious situation and he prayed he could make it off the ship. Captain Kuznetsky's insistence made it all too clear. Roman had no way of knowing what really lay behind all the lingering stares he had received from the crew. But, Roman thought, no matter. The captain obviously knew more than he was telling, and his warning gave Roman no choice.

Roman opened the door to find Seaman Shopaloff waiting. He gave Roman a sad nod and indicated they needed to move quickly. They hurried to Roman's cabin. He hastily packed his necessary possessions into his duffle bag and Shopaloff led him quickly and silently back toward the deck. They stood still, scarcely breathing, in the corridor at the entrance to the deck for several minutes before venturing out. The distance to the gangplank seemed unimaginably long and dangerous. How can I leave the ship unnoticed? Whoever is out there in the shadows is probably my enemy.

The crew, fully awake now in the drab morning daylight, clustered here and there in small groups, chatting, looking around. No one was about his regular duties and no officers were in sight.

Roman started to step forward when a body moved out of the shadows and blocked his way. "Where'd you thing you're goin', spy?" came a voice. Immediately a hand and then an arm appeared yanking the voice out of sight back into the darkness away from Roman.

Taking a deep breath, with eyes straight ahead and legs feeling rubbery, Roman walked with Shopaloff at his side to the gangway leading down to the pier. He forced himself not to panic or hurry; nor did he nod to the few men whom he passed directly. There was no further trouble.

As if he weren't already the center of attention because of the suspicions, he felt all eyes on him as he stepped across the gunwale onto the gangway in the pre-dawn darkness. He was carrying his bag, which pointed even more attention to the fact that he was leaving. On the pier, Shopaloff handed Roman his duffle bag and touched his arm in a sign of affection and whispered, "I'll miss you. Go with God, young friend."

Roman's confidence was shattered with vivid images of what might happen. He thought the worst. Would he be attacked, picked up and thrown into the water? Would they come after him? They might even shoot him in the back at any moment.

Nothing happened as Roman walked briskly toward Sevastopol gripping his bag so tightly his fingers ached. He walked with determination, as though he had some destination. Actually, he hadn't thought that far ahead. He was breathing hard. The air was cold and the wind chilling. His shoes crunched on the crisp fallen leaves, but he wasn't even aware of the weather. Uppermost in his mind, as he hurried away from the *Empress Catherine*, was that Capt. Kuznetsky had given him his life in allowing him to leave the ship.

Whenever the *Empress Maria* had been in port, Roman had spent most of his time reading in the ship's library, studying or writing to Xenia; he seldom went ashore. The town held nothing of interest for him. Now, he had to leave the *Empress Catherine* and wanted desperately to hide, to run somewhere. But where? He was simply adrift, unwelcome aboard any ship, a fugitive from the only life he knew, the only career he wanted.

Most of all, Roman felt thoroughly isolated right now as never before—removed from everyone he knew, including his family.

He walked and walked. He had to get away from the ship, but he didn't know where to go. As Roman rummaged through his mind on what to do, he suddenly thought: Volodya! He remembered where his friend's mother lived. He must tell her of the tragedy. He had accompanied Volodya there one day and suddenly realized that her tiny apartment was one of the very few places in Sevastopol that he did know. The realization energized him, so he stepped forward more purposely toward the edge of town away from the harbor. Does she know her son is dead?

The thought of having to bring her such tragic news cramped his stomach and dried his tongue to the roof of his mouth. Is there any news in the world worse than telling a mother her child had died? Could I tell her that Volodya had taken his own life? Will I have that kind of strength? Then he realized he would have to tell about the Czar, too. With all he had to say, unless he told some terrible lie, it surely would end up terrifying the poor woman. As he walked, he kept refining what he would say. But no matter how he phrased it, it was still the same paralyzing news. Volodya is dead, Mrs. Fock!

***

Short of his destination, Roman stopped abruptly in the middle of the street. I must find some other place to go. Where? Maybe I should talk to someone on Admiral Kolchak's staff. Surely, someone there will realize an officer's life—my life—is at stake aboard the *Empress Catherine*. Someone should know what to do.

Roman hesitated before turning around. Yes. Admiral Kolchak's headquarters were just down the next block. Roman headed that way, walking quickly now. He realized more clearly with each step that he was highly visible on the street in the early morning light. There were no shadows where he could hide: no place to take cover. News of the tragedy aboard the *Empress Catherine* could be known by now. Certainly, the abdication of the Czar would be public. Most everyone would surely know.

Roman rounded the corner and spotted Admiral Kolchak's headquarters only a few doors down. His flag was hanging out in front.

He went in and saw a lieutenant sitting at a desk. He stood at the counter that separated the entrance from the working area until the officer looked up from what he was reading. He stood, and slowly came over to Roman.

"Yes, Lieutenant, what is it?"

Roman felt the man's arrogance and knew he would not be of

much help. But, he had to ask, no matter what kind of man the officer was. He explained himself—all the while realizing that the officer was looking at him dumbly. Finished at last, Roman stood there waiting for some reply while trying to appear respectful and calm.

When it came, it numbed Roman. "I'm sorry, Lieutenant. The way things are, there is no place I can send you safely." The lieutenant moved closer to the counter and leaned towards Roman. His next words were more kindly, but Roman read the fear clearly in them. "Really, I can't help you. I wish I could, but I just don't know." He stopped, helpless. "Admiral Kolchak is on the *Empress Catherine* at this moment. Matters there are out of hand. The abdication of the Czar has changed everything. We don't..." He stopped again.

"Lieutenant, I shouldn't be telling you this, you understand? But your life is in your own hands now. The Imperial Russian Navy is...under... mutiny. We are all in great danger. I'm sorry, Lieutenant." The lieutenant looked into Roman's crestfallen face, and then turned away, running a hand through his hair.

Roman was shocked to learn that Admiral Kolchak was aboard the Empress Catherine, where he had just come from. So, the Admiral must already know of my predicament.

He turned and hurried back out into the street. Walking quickly, he headed once again to Volodya's mother's place. As he neared her home, he kept pondering how he would tell her, but he never found a satisfactory way. The terrible picture of Volodya was constantly in his mind, and how he had so closely missed stopping his friend's hand. He could still hear the pistol shot in his memory as it echoed over and over. I just have to tell her and help her as best I can.

He stepped to the door of her lodgings and knocked. He managed a smile as she opened the door. She seemed surprised to find him standing there so early in the day but she said, "Come in, come in, Roman. I am so glad to see you." She waved him inside.

Mrs. Fock was a tiny woman, with bright eyes set into a face woven with wrinkles. Her gray hair was caught up imperfectly in a bun, strands hanging down over her ears. Aware of her appearance she brought a hand up to her hair and fussed with it futilely, then shook her head and mumbled something, but continued to usher him in. A widow, she lived alone. Her husband had been in command of an infantry unit when he was killed months ago. She had another son fighting on the German front. She had moved to this tiny, two-room apartment belonging to relatives in order to be closer to Volodya. She felt it was safer here than nearer the German front. Her belongings filled most of the area, allowing Roman little room to maneuver.

"How is Volodya? Tell me. I moved here to be closer to him, but I never see him anyway. The war... The war is never kind. Families do not matter."

Roman stood there tongue-tied, while she chattered pleasantly on. But he couldn't postpone his message. He must give this fragile little woman the terrible news.

Mrs. Fock continued. "Sit down, Roman. Please. Be comfortable. You look very tired. Things are not..." She paused. She looked at Roman's face and realized something was wrong. "Roman? Volodya...is he....?"

Roman's voice croaked as he gushed out the news. "...Dead, Mrs. Fock. Volodya is dead. He died during the night." With a groan she fell to the floor before Roman could catch her. He lifted her into an overstuffed chair and kept his arms around her as she swayed back and forth, moaning softly. There were no tears, just her moaning; her face captured in pain, the wrinkles deepening as her sorrow swept through her. Then she stiffened and sat upright, the momentary weakness suddenly gone. Now a tear came, sliding slowly down her cheek, unnoticed, to stop by the corner of her mouth.

"Yes? And how?" she whispered, her eyes wide open, asking almost matter-of-factly.

Then came the hardest words Roman had ever spoken—words he had never thought he would utter—to explain what had happened. He tried but couldn't soften the story of Volodya's passionate suicide, and the subsequent suspicions that he and Volodya were spies. Volodya's mother listened silently and painfully to every word, but then a strange, wonderful comfort reflected on her face. Truth seemed to have a supreme liberating quality and she recognized he was telling her the truth.

"Thank you, Roman, for coming." She had stoically accepted the inevitable implications. "So, the Czar is dead. The monarchy's tyranny is gone. But, no. Not really, eh? Now, a new kind of tyranny. The people's tyranny of revenge, eh? Yes. The people will want revenge for all the years of injustice and hardship. But there never will be enough. Blood thirsts on blood." Sensing Roman's predicament, she paused. "And you? Are you here because you cannot stay aboard your ship?"

Roman nodded.

"But you are not a spy either. Volodya was not... Nor are you."

Roman nodded again at her words. The truth of his own situation kept becoming more and more evident and the danger he was in loomed ever greater in his mind.

"All right, I will move out," she said in her matter-of-fact manner. "I have friends I can stay with. You stay here. There is food for several days. You will be safe. No one saw you come?'

"I don't think so."

"Good. You will be all right here. Don't go outside. I will check on you." She gripped his arm fiercely. "Thank you for coming. Thank you for telling me the truth."

Then she stood up with surprising strength and busied herself around the room, hurriedly grabbing some clothes and some small packages of food. "There is plenty more."

She went to the door and turned to him. "You are a good man, Roman Sturmer. May God deal well with you. Thank you again." She sought no further comfort, having brought herself firmly, stoically, under control the way strong women manage to do. Then she opened the door, pulled her coat close against the cold and was gone before Roman could help her. The mist concealed her as she quickly disappeared into the drab neighborhood.

***

The next day a friend of Volodya's, Peter Zolotuhin, came to the house. Roman was surprised to see him as he had been with him in the navigating division on the *Empress Catherine*.

"Peter! How did you find me?"

"Roman!" Peter was just as surprised. "I was hunting for Volodya's mother. And I find you instead."

"Come in quickly. Did anyone see you coming here?"

"I don't think so. I did not see anyone following me. Where is Volodya's mother?" Peter looked around the room as he entered.

"With friends. She has let me have her place for a while."

Peter's friend was obviously relieved. "May I stay with you? They are looking for me, too."

Dread sliced through Roman, icy cold. "You? What did you do?"

"I don't know. I can only guess that it's because I was a friend of Volodya's. That was why Capt. Kuznetsky warned you. Because you are...were...a friend of Volodya's. His roommate. Everyone...well, the crewmen...think he was a German spy. The night before the *Empress Maria* blew up they had seen Volodya at the gun turrets. They think he sabotaged them."

"But he was inspecting them!" interrupted Roman. "That is what he was supposed to do! He was on duty, doing what he was ordered to do!"

"I know. I know, Roman. It's crazy. Everything is crazy now because the Czar has abdicated! I hear that in Petrograd things are much worse than here. Strikes and riots. People killed. Officers being murdered!" With that Roman silently wondered about Xenia.

"Well, we can do nothing to change all that. We are being hunted, all right. We'd better stay here out of sight for a while."

The two stayed there for several days before they happened to learn that Volodya had been taken from the ship to Sevastopol's hospital even though he had been dead on arrival. No one knew what to do with his body. For some reason—because he was considered a German spy—sailors wouldn't let anyone bury him.

When Volodya' mother came by to check on Roman, he and Peter told her about Volodya's body which deepened the grief she was already suffering. Couldn't something be done? He couldn't just be left there like that, to rot, unburied. So, the three sat down to make plans.

Roman and Peter had been at the house six or seven days when one morning they managed to sneak their way to the hospital without being discovered. They looked furtively around corners and stayed on abandoned streets. Luckily, Peter discovered he knew a couple of the hospital aides. Keeping a low profile, Peter and Roman persuaded them to let them steal Volodya's body and quickly take it to the cemetery. Mrs. Fock and a few other family members arranged with cemetery officials for permission to bury him. The burial was a simple, hurried affair in one of the less noticeable corners of the graveyard on a freezing late March morning, gray with winter's dreariness. Roman was hesitant to be of much help because of his German name, so he remained in the background as much as possible.

It was 1917 and Russia was total chaos.

Volodya's mother was extremely grateful for their help and offered her lodgings to them for as long as they wanted. Roman and Peter thanked her but declined. They had been talking about their situation for days and thought for a while it would be worth the risk to attempt to see Admiral Kolchak and seek help—or do whatever their higher officers commanded. But—upon the realization that the former crew of the Empress Maria was now on the Empress Catherine, the very men both Roman and Peter wanted least to see them, they changed their minds.

They walked unobtrusively as possible to Admiral Kolchak's headquarters and requested that the lieutenant on duty somehow get a message to the Admiral. They finally persuaded him, and soon they were ordered to go to the *Empress Maria's* second sister ship, the *Emperor Alexander III*. It was still under construction in the shipyards at Nikolayev, farther north on the Black Sea. The officer's strategy for sending them there was that none of the former crew of the *Empress Maria* had been sent to Nikolayev, as far as anyone seemed to know. Confusing as it was, chances were that none of the *Emperor Alexander III's* crew were aware, yet, of the suspicions about Roman and Peter. They should be safe there. The officers were wrong.

Chapter 12

The train transporting Roman and Peter crept along to Nikolayev, the naval shipyards northwest of Sevastopol. They would have made it faster going by ship—but they had no choice: they were on the run. What took three days of travel would normally take less than a day. But these times were far from normal.

Russia's turmoil in April of 1917 was greater with two wars on its hands. The Great War itself was now a lost cause because Russia had long since lost its ability to cope. Thousands of soldiers deserted daily. They wandered around: dejected, with no job, no food. The monarchy had crumbled since the Czar's abdication. Russia was paralyzed. Every effort to create a government body only seemed to be without organization making matters worse.

Transportation was an unimaginable mess of chaos. Trains blocked trains so that food could not get to the starving people in the cities. Railroad tracks were clogged for miles. Roman and Peter waited repeatedly for their train to move from one village to the next, dreading what they might encounter. The political situation appeared more sinister daily, and the two of them saw this personally. The mutiny of ships' crews in the Black Sea affected them. Military authority was shattered.

Roman and Peter repeatedly glanced furtively over their shoulders for anyone paying them undue attention. They had heard that death squads were murdering officers. In their black uniforms, with their service caps off and tucked in their pockets, they still gave off the "air" of officers with their straight posture and quick steps. They finally found a railroad car in which to ride. It was almost totally filled with peasants, the elderly, and young children, all eyeing them curiously—

and they felt, suspiciously.

At last Nikolayev. Roman and Peter straightened their stance once again. Eyes straight ahead, they walked briskly to the hulk of the *Emperor Alexander III* where workmen were putting finishing touches on her. Without any interference, Roman and Peter found that the ship's quarters seemed available enough, ready to occupy, so they went directly to the captain. He was a man Roman had never seen before. Peter waited outside while Roman cautiously entered the office. He saluted and said, "Sir, I am Lieutenant Roman Sturmer reporting for duty aboard your ship."

The captain looked at him and replied, "My friend, you had better go see the chairman of the ship's committee. They're running this ship now."

Those ominous words startled Roman. They had hoped conditions would be better here than in Sevastopol, but apparently not. Roman found Peter and together they sought out the ship's committee. Roman recognized the man sitting at the largest of several tables set up together in the officers' wardroom. He was a non-commissioned officer whom Roman remembered from the *Empress Maria*. He had been one of the gunners in the turret Roman had commanded. "Hello, Vantz," he greeted

"Hello, Sturmer," Herbert Vantz replied noncommittally, while eyeing him carefully. If he was surprised to see Sturmer this far from Sevastopol, he gave no indication. Roman was aware that Vantz had not included Roman's rank in his greeting. Just "Sturmer." This blunt greeting sent a chill through Roman.

"I've been assigned to this ship," Roman continued calmly. "The Captain told me to report to you."

Vantz stared at him silently for a long moment before replying officiously, "We know you very well, Sturmer. You are a good man. We went through the explosion on the *Maria* together." What he said next, though, sent even colder chills through Roman. "But you have a German name. I've heard that all officers with German names in Sevastopol are being executed." Roman held back a gasp of dismay and waited.

After another lengthy silence, Vantz continued expressing little emotion. "So we'll send a telegram to see if this is true. If it is true, we will kill you. If it is not true, we will be very happy to work with you." Roman could barely control his rush of anger—and fear—at the man's pitiless tone.

Vantz paid him no more attention but turned to Peter Zolotuhin and questioned him. He seemed to recognize him, but on hearing his name dismissed him with, "What I told Sturmer applies only to him. We will deal with you in a moment."

Roman steeled himself to keep his face straight. This was not the same Vantz he had known aboard the *Empress Maria*. How could a man change so quickly?

Vantz was wielding life-and-death power over Roman, his recent superior officer, as matter-of-factly as if drinking a cup of tea. Roman had never treated Vantz with even the slightest show of contempt or arrogance. Yet, Vantz sat there now, implacably judging Roman as if he had committed some great crime. His actions told Roman just how bitter this revolutionary wildness had become. How could things change so quickly? It's worse than I thought. Up to now, despite all that had happened, Roman had held a small measure of disbelief about all the turmoil, that it was somehow being exaggerated by what people were saying. But there was no mistaking the lethal import of Vantz's words. Even the slightest indication of Roman's inner anger could bring much greater danger to himself and Peter. Ironically Peter was not affected, because his name was clearly not German.

Roman stood there a moment to get himself under control. *My life is in great jeopardy. Vantz must know what I'm going through. How else would a man react to such judgment?*

Reeling internally from the conversation, all he said to Vantz was, "Very well," and turned around and walked away. Peter stayed behind to answer Vantz. Roman went back to the room he and Peter had been assigned and sat on the edge of the bunk, allowing all the events of the last few weeks to settle on him like a shroud. He felt defeated. *God… my dream. Is this how my career in the Navy is to end? I've been on active duty for a mere nine months. Is my career over?*

It hadn't even been a year since Roman had first stepped aboard the *Empress Maria*. He wondered what his naval career had been anyway... a few engagements on the Empress Maria before it blew up, Volodya's suicide, himself under suspicion of spying. Now he was on the run... from whom? It was hard to believe that even sailors were crazed by the fever of revolution, out to tear society apart. What now?

Sitting on his bunk, alone, he prayed and searched for some way of escape. He knew he couldn't keep waiting while these people, these crewmen, became his executioners.

Roman nervously waited for Peter to show up, but he never did. Where is he?" he puzzled. He couldn't do anything about it, except hope his friend was all right.

Finally Roman went back to the captain and told him of his conversation with Vantz and asked the captain to let him go ashore. His plan was to somehow reach his father. He'd heard his father was now Commander of a regiment near Moscow and he knew how to find him—if he could get away unnoticed.

The captain disappointed him. "This is war," he said, "and I have no right to grant you such permission."

"What shall I do?" Roman asked.

"Go to the Admiral of Nikolayev and ask him. He has the authority to grant such a request."

Roman quickly followed that advice. Admiral Andriy Pokrovsky was a three-star officer and Roman was surprised at how old he appeared to be. After saluting, and giving his name, he explained simply, "I need to leave. They are planning to kill me."

The admiral gave him an answer—one he had heard before. "This is war. I have no right to let you go."

Roman could not contain himself and he let loose some of his anger. "But I am only 21! You're an old man! You've had years in the navy..." he blurted then realized what he'd said. That such bluntness could slip out seemed incredible later, but at the time those two ages were the most relevant facts in the world.

Roman must have touched a sensitive spot because the admiral replied, "We'll send a telegram to Admiral Kolchak. " Now, in desperation Roman argued more fervently than ever informing him that the ship's committee had already sent a telegram, nearly two hours ago. And a reply would come to that before any reply would come to Admiral Pokrovksy. *So what is the use of the Admiral even sending a telegram?* Roman thought to himself, *I might be dead by the time permission comes to give me leave.*

For half an hour Roman pressed his case knowing he was running out of time. Finally, the admiral gave him permission. Roman headed for a train as fast as he could, praying he could disappear from town before the ship's committee could find him. Where is Peter? Will I live to see Xenia? Or my family?

Chapter 13

The trip by train to see his father seemed to on go forever. Roman felt it rather like the trip he and Peter had taken from Sevastopol north to Nikolayev—endless jerking; delays throughout the days and nights— with cars full of haggard and weary people staring suspiciously at him. It was impossible to sleep. Most of his time was spent standing with one shoulder pressed against a corridor wall. By stooping, he could see through the dirty train window. The sight was unfamiliar in that it no longer looked like the Russia he loved. Although it was late April, dirty snow still covered the ground as winter retreated reluctantly from these parts of Russia.

Three or four days after leaving Nikolayev, Roman located his father's headquarters in Torzhok, a small town northwest of Moscow. He'd heard that his father was now commanding several units of cavalry which were each split into two battalions: one unit in Torso, the other in a town a few miles away.

Roman was so exhausted that when the train finally arrived in Torso, he departed the train on unsteady feet. When he learned he had to walk quite a distance to his father's regimental headquarters, he took a deep breath, telling himself, I've come this far, I can make it.

A wide-eyed stare and raised eyebrows greeted him as he finally entered his father's office.

"Teapot!" his father called out heartily. Roman grinned at his father's use of his favorite childhood name. "What are you doing here?" He strode across the room and grabbed Roman in a bear hug, then held him at arm's length while looking closely at his son's face. "You look very tired, Roman. What has been happening down in the Black Sea?"

Roman started to tell him, but his father interrupted, "I am so glad to see you, but I am very busy right now and have to go. You wait here. Make yourself comfortable and I will be back as soon as I can. We can talk then." He patted Roman's shoulder as he crossed the room to shrug himself into his greatcoat while hurrying from the room.

Watching him go, Roman thought that his father looked thinner, and tired, too. What is he going through?

When his father had stood before him with his hands on his shoulders, Roman was an inch or so taller than his father. He'd never realized that before. *Have I grown or has he shrunk? Father seems smaller, and quite haggard. He must be facing some difficult problems—just as I am.* Roman felt not so much the son any more, but his father's equal: two men under great pressures. The war wreaked havoc on everyone.

A well-worn sofa in the office welcomed Roman after the fatiguing train journey. He fell asleep almost instantly. When he awoke, it was dark outside, and someone—probably an orderly—had lit a gas lamp in the room. Whoever had done so had also placed his greatcoat over him to offset the chill in the room.

As he sat up, rubbing a hand over his face, the door opened and his father entered. "Ah-ha. I see you made good use of your time," his father said as he shrugged himself out of his own greatcoat and took off his overshoes. He seemed in good spirits, but as Roman became more awake and studied his father, he could see fatigue and tension still lining his features.

"Come, let's have some tea. I need to warm up." He rang a bell on the table serving as his desk and ordered tea for them.

Turning back to Roman, he said, "So, tell me, why are you here, so far from your ship?"

Roman explained his situation while his father listened intently, showing great concern as he heard the details. "The Czar's abdication has done great damage to Russia," he said to Roman. "We are no longer the same nation. I don't know the solution or even how we've allowed it to happen." He just kept shaking his head in amazement.

"How are you Father?"

His father threw up his hands and responded with a great chuckle, "You will not believe me, but what I tell you is all true. Every word—I'm not exaggerating. There is an officer in one of the two close battalions who has loudly expressed suspicion about names and accuses me of being a German spy!"

How similar! It was an even more incredible charge than what had been lodged against Roman. But, even though it was so outlandish, it posed considerable danger.

"It wasn't too widely believed. On the contrary, most of the men didn't believe it, and took measures to protect me. However, the two battalions in the far town had heard rumor that the two nearest were holding me prisoner because they thought me a German spy! They didn't believe such charges and they were in route to attack that village to rescue me. By a strange quirk of circumstances, the nearer battalion heard of the eminent attack. But what they heard was that the other battalion was coming to capture me.

"While the whole situation was comic, it was also potentially tragic. I had to straighten out both groups of battalions. I was the only man either side would listen to. But whether I could stop all of those loyal people before they killed each other needlessly over me was another question."

"I had to ride my horse between the two groups. 'Stop!' I cried. 'Stop! I'm all right'." The two men laughed at the unbelievable tale that had turned out so favorably. It crossed Roman's mind that it would be one of the unwritten battles of the war and the revolution.

After his father finished his story, he looked intently at Roman and asked, "What do you want?" His voice reflected his concern. "Are you alright?"

Roman didn't know what he wanted except to get out of the terrible predicament he was in. There was no way his story could possibly have a happy ending like his father's.

"I don't know," Roman said. "I really want everything to be different, but that's a childish wish."

"Yes. Well, we can do nothing tonight. Both of us are very tired. A good night's sleep will help us to find an answer."

The next day everything remained unresolved. Roman stayed with his father for several days until a telegram arrived from a friend of Roman's in Nikolayev. It said only "Come back." The two words were foreboding, but Roman knew he could do only one thing: return or be considered a deserter.

Roman returned in early May with increasing anxiety. The two-word telegram ordering him to "come back" had told him nothing—good or bad—about his status with the crew of the *Emperor Alexander III*. What had been the reply to the telegram the ship's committee had sent? Would there be some remarkable reprieve? Roman shied away from answering his own question. He felt he was heading back to his own execution.

Roman had no anchor other than his loyalty to the Navy.

As he sat on the slow train between Moscow and Nikolayev listening to the clacking wheels on the tracks, he rested on that anchor – loyalty. If not for that, what was left? Of the Navy? Or the Army, or anything else that was Russia? Xenia? Without the Czar to serve, with only a bunch of men who had violently taken authority unto themselves—and who stood for what?—What choices did he have? Roman asked himself that question over and over as he stood at the end of one of the two crowded passenger cars. Only loyalty provided an answer that held any honorable meaning. In the end, though, arguing with himself on such a philosophical plan was worthless. All the high-sounding words and phrases amounted to just that, words and phrases. They left him in a deeper quandary than ever. I can't run, but how can I save myself?

Even as he asked that, his father's reassuring words came back to him. "Things truly were in the hands of God."

Roman had not heard his father speak such words often. He knew his father had religious feelings, but they were not discussed openly, simply understood. The family was Orthodox as most of Russia was. His father had gone with them to church, when he could, at one of the churches near where they had been living at the time. Roman's mother's faith was an open tangible thing on the other hand; she spoke of her feelings frequently and freely. The family's attendance at church on Sundays and always at special seasons was expected. His father's words had a calming effect, and in a way brought them closer. Roman did not know what he would face. But, yes, his fate was out of his hands and in God's. That thought lingered and brought him a sense of peace.

He thought of other times when he must have been in God's hands… when he was rescued after sliding down the barnacled hull of the *Empress Maria*, for instance. Why didn't I drown? And so, now as he stood in the crush of the train crowd, he knew he could not just submit himself to the whims of sailors who were caught up in the violence of the revolution. This madness must only be a temporary spasm; such wildness can't continue for long. Still…I don't have any other options aside from reporting back to the *Emperor Alexander III*…do I? Nothing acceptable came to mind.

To be a deserter is unthinkable.

Chapter 14

Fear escorted Roman as he reported back to the ship as requested. But, he was met with the most inexplicable behavior he'd ever encountered— even more surprising than Chairman Vantz's ominous sentence days earlier.

Roman made his appearance before the ship's committee, but not one word was mentioned about any telegram sent or received, about his being a German spy, or about any execution of officers with German names. Nothing. Not a word. It was as though he had walked into a totally different world, except for the presence of the ship's committee and Chairman Vantz.

Vantz himself greeted Roman as though nothing amiss had occurred between them. There was no continuity to anything—not even apologies to him for terrifying him with threats of execution. Roman was greeted cordially, matter-of-factly, with the same attitude as had existed on the *Empress Maria* prior to the explosion seven months before.

Equally strange was that nobody seemed to care anymore about the Great War. Fighting still continued; but Germany, Austria and Turkey seemed to have faded into insignificance. Almost comical in the face of things was that Roman was elected secretary of the ship's committee! Instead of being their enemy, I'm now one of them! How can this be?

Baffled as he was by this turn of events, Roman was cautious about questioning anything. He hoped his great relief wasn't revealed on his face. If this is some kind of game, I can play as well as Vantz and the rest of them.

Roman's new ranking lasted barely longer than a flash of

lightning. In as bizarre an act as his appointment had been, he was fired after his third meeting as secretary. The reason given: he took the minutes of the meetings too efficiently! Roman wrote so quickly that he was able to put down nearly verbatim everything everyone said—but no one believed that any committee member could have said such stupid things. When he read out the minutes, great arguments, denials and accusations, broke out, all of which ultimately landed on Roman's head. No one accepted the responsibility for having said what Roman wrote down. So, obviously, he must be wrong. It did not endear him to the committee, but it did not do any great harm to the new-felt sense of peace, if that was the word, that reigned on the *Emperor Alexander III*.

***

Roman's commanding officer gave him a new assignment. "Take one of the ship's small sailing boats and seek food for the crew in the nearby coastal villages." For days he foraged—from village to village—gathering and bringing back his meager gleanings. Everyone was hungry. A sense of futility weighed on him.

The unpleasant job continued until the day of testing the *Emperor Alexander III* at sea. The crew was ordered to take the ship to Sevastopol. But once in Sevastopol, they didn't go to sea: they just waited. Whatever the reasons for this, Roman didn't find out, because other matters intruded, matters which brought the whole situation of sailors versus officers to the surface.

Roman's fears of Vantz's ultimatum, which by now seemed as though it had never happened, were refueled. The weather was extremely cold—it was now almost November, 1917. During the summer and fall the situation in Petrograd had continued to deteriorate. When the *Alexander III* arrived in Sevastopol, matters were noticeably worse. Men who called themselves "commissars" arrived in the city from the Baltic Sea, boasting that they had been killing officers everywhere, but it had not happened in Sevastopol. Why not, they wanted to know?

Orders were given to begin murdering officers whom they

remembered from as far back as the uprisings more than a dozen years earlier. "It's all necessary," they claimed. "Kill the officers and take their bodies to Malahov Hill, the local cemetery." How many they actually killed nobody knew, but the former officers of the *Emperor Alexander III* and the *Empress Catherine* were under great tension when one from their company quietly disappeared. Each officer spent his days wondering if he would be the next target. It was a time of great despair.

Fear was an ever-present companion.

***

Roman, a deck officer, and his roommate, Victor Neholosheff, an engineering officer, heard crews haranguing officers one night; their voices drifting clearly into their cabin from the deck above through the open overhead skylight. These arguments were continuously fueled by the commissars from the Baltic. Roman and Victor looked at each other and puzzled, "What is going on?"

The debate went on into the wee hours of the November morning. The engineering crew said they liked their officers and would not kill them, but they would kill the deck officers, the gunnery and navigating officers. The deck and gunnery crews said they liked their officers but would be willing to kill the engineering officers.

And so it went, Sturmer and Victor listened intently as to how the men above would decide their fate. They both felt the end was near and an attack on them was eminent. Roman even went so far as to write Xenia a farewell letter telling her how much he cared for her. It was so sad it brought him to the verge of tears—but he never got to mail it. Catastrophic events were changing Russia forever and the turmoil continued to grip the country. Without a monarch, the monarchy itself was dead.

Roman and his fellow officers realized they were in serious jeopardy from that moment on: They could read the change in their crews and among the people beyond. They kept as close an ear as possible to the chaos and destructive events occurring in Petrograd and Moscow as news reached them. For Roman and others who had loved ones in those cities this was especially painful.

Roman was concerned he'd had no word from Xenia for months. He knew nothing of the possible hardships she and her family might have suffered. He knew nothing about both her and her father having been in prison for three months; nothing about families leaving Moscow for who knows where? He longed for news of home and then, unexpectedly, he received a letter from his sister Kira.

He read that the whole family was well and safe and hoping to be together right after Christmas in Torsok. Relieved, Roman knew that he would go no matter what trouble he would have to endure to get to the reunion. He needed time with Xenia. His pulse became rapid as he made his decision. *I must go regardless of the consequences.*

Christmas in Russia

In the time of the czars, Christmas Day was celebrated on December 25 and was one of the holiest days of the year in the Russian Orthodox Church. It celebrated the birth of Jesus and the Christian heritage.

This season, Sviatki, also brought out the very popular custom of mumming in the 1800's. The high-spirits of the mummers, dressed in colorful costumes, added to the Sviatki with peasants and aristocrats alike joining together briefly in a joyous time. The frosty air rang with merriment as Troikas, lightweight sleighs generally pulled by three horses, filled with merrymakers skimmed across the ice and snow to numerous country dances and feasts.

Trees were decorated and gifts exchanged during this season which lasted through January 7th. Every day during the Holy Season the Church held special services and prior to Christmas Day certain foods were avoided. On Christmas Eve, starting at 6 o'clock and lasting for several hours, nearly everyone attended church. Candles glowed, singing filled churches, and Communion was served as a traditional part of the Orthodox ceremony. In those days the weak, and even the pregnant stood. The services were not meant to be "enjoyed". Today benches are placed around the walls and those individuals are allowed to sit.

Traditional feasts on Christmas Day in Russia brought extended families together. It was a time of special delicacies such as piroshki, blini, borscht with sour cream, jellied sturgeon, caviar and an abundance of tea and vodka.

During the reign of Nicholas II, the last czar, Russia encompassed areas that included any Slavic nationality groups. So Christmas combined both Russian Orthodox and Slavic customs.

It was a holy time, but generally light-hearted. Christmas carols, Kolyadki, were sung and neighbors were treated to bags of sweets.

Girls of marriageable age loved to guess who their future husband would be by using many rituals and imaginable methods. In many cases Christian customs were superimposed over old pagan customs.

Arts, including the written works, flourished, but by the turn of the century conditions were changing and industrialization was increasing. Much of the population was poor and starving. Discontent increased. In 1905 unarmed workers protested to the czar that reform was needed and by 1917 the czar was overthrown. Christianity and Christmas became suppressed. It was no longer the joyous season observed in the traditional manner and disobedience was very dangerous. The legendary Grandfather Frost tradition with his bag of gifts continued. During the Soviet period the red suit was changed to a blue one. The holy family of Jesus, Mary, and Joseph was largely replaced by Grandfather Frost, the Snow Maiden, and the New Year's Boy.

Chapter 15

It was already January 1918, when Roman received his sister Kira's letter saying he should come home for the reunion at the home in Torzhok. Roman read most closely the last part of her letter that informed him he should make every effort to come because of a young lady who would be staying with them. She didn't mention the young lady's name. It wasn't necessary!

While Roman was struggling with the cold, miserable days that encompassed the Black Sea area, he read that the winter was crisp and beautiful in Torzhok with temperatures ranging from 20 to 30 degrees below zero. Great amounts of frost and snow covered the ground, Kira wrote. She stressed that their father's sleigh would certainly be available whenever he and the young lady wanted to use it!

Roman visualized showing Xenia the beauty of Torzhok. The city—an ancient trade route renowned for its gold embroidery—was about 150 miles north of Moscow.

Such an invitation could not be ignored.

Roman's thoughts of Xenia had increasingly filled his mind these days. He hadn't heard from her for several months, nor had he written her, with all the strange circumstances aboard the *Alexander III* pressing so heavily on him. Since November's terrifying events had changed Russia drastically—especially the past weeks—he was now more worried than ever about his family and Xenia. *Will she be happy to see me? How has all of the chaos and upheaval in Petrograd and Moscow touched her?*

The reports coming from those areas could no longer be considered exaggerated; they were too shattering. The Bolsheviks had finally taken the great step and attacked the Winter Palace, declaring themselves the new government of Russia. Lenin, Trotsky and other newcomers were Russia's leaders now.

Naval personnel in the Black Sea listened with utmost attention to the news that even some of the naval forces in Petrograd had joined the attack: the cruiser *Aurora* had even fired on the Winter Palace. The fact that the ship's gunners had fired only blanks didn't make significant difference. The point was that a unit of the Imperial Russian Navy had fired on its own government in rebellion.

Roman was totally disheartened. *Now, there was no turning back. The Revolution! It has come at last. Violence is the ruling power.*

The Bolsheviks made it clear there would be no limits to the violence they were ready and willing to wreak in order to establish themselves in a position of power. Yet, despite the terror accompanying the news, word of the Revolution was met with cheers from the ships' committees.

Roman knew that Xenia had been in medical school in Petrograd, much too close to all of the horrendous events. He *must* see for himself that she was all right. He *had* to go to the reunion. His superior officer, a lieutenant acting as his superior at any rate, refused Roman's request for ten days leave. The request was then directed to the ship's committee. He didn't get permission from them either. When that didn't happen, he chose the only course open to him: leave without permission, a serious offense. Absence without leave was the most serious of military misbehavior aside from outright desertion.

Regardless of the consequences, Roman packed and left Sevastopol for Torso.

***

Roman managed to get aboard a train to Moscow and squeeze into a compartment meant for four passengers. Due to the continuing confusion and incredible crowding, eight people were already occupying the space. His uneasiness increased when he overheard that some officers from his squadron were also on the train, even a lieutenant from the *Alexander III*. Those officers had permission to go to a conference in Petrograd for gunnery officers. Their own passes as well as passes for some of their wives were good through Moscow and beyond.

Roman was uneasy. He had nothing to support his presence on the train.

In Roman's heavily crowded compartment, the travelers were forced to squeeze into any and every available crevice. He ended up on the compartment's berth, sandwiched amidst half a dozen other men. As soldiers boarded the train authoritatively demanding people to show their documents, one of Roman's "neighbors"—as he called the others on the berth—told the soldiers to leave some passengers alone, because they had proper documents. Then this "neighbor" motioned toward Roman, "Here's a man without documents. Take him," he said sarcastically.

Because of the way they were positioned, Roman desperately nudged him in the head with his foot in an attempt to silence the "neighbor". Fortunately the man realized his mistake before the soldiers did anything and said no more. Roman breathed a sigh of relief when the train started to pull away and the soldiers had to jump from the car and disappeared. Roman knew how close he had come to the last moment of his life; they would have shot him outside the train. Once again, Roman realized God was watching out for him.

The train was safe until nearing Moscow and there was no further trouble with check points beyond. Roman chose to get off a little farther from Moscow and change trains to one going to the station nearest home. There he was met and hugged by his family and saw a smiling Xenia. She was beautifully dressed and the hood of her dark green cape was trimmed in white fur, accenting the joyful expression on her face.

At last! She seems so happy to see me! She's beautiful. Roman had waited so long to see her that he held out his arms to her and gave her a big hug. Roman realized at that moment how much he loved Xenia and rejoiced that she hugged him back.

Time was spent with the family and enjoying the picturesque city. Finally, later that day, he managed to have some time alone with Xenia and told her of his love. Nervously, he asked her to marry him. She unhesitatingly said, "Yes." Roman was overjoyed.

When Roman announced their engagement at dinner that evening, there was much excitement. The family adored Xenia and loudly expressed their pleasure. The war problems were shoved aside for the moment and it became a time of joyfulness and celebration in his father's house. Amid the holiday decorations they toasted the couple with a cup of wine—which was very rare in those days—followed by coffee, and a beautifully decorated dessert. To Roman it seemed like a dream and his situation was temporarily forgotten.

Kira had been right. A heavy layer of snow covered the frozen ground giving Roman and Xenia an excuse to make use of the horse-drawn sleigh. During this time alone, snuggled deep in heavy carriage robes, they brought each other up to date over their months apart.

"Oh, Roman!" Xenia whispered as she hugged him and snuggled deeper into the heavy blankets covering everything but their noses. Basking in Roman's formal proposal, in public (so to speak), before his whole family, she was so happy. Now, she whispered, "You must talk to my father. Ask him for permission." That went without saying. It was an ancient tradition.

But, as they brought each other up to date, Xenia was visibly upset when Roman told of his experiences of being on-the-run since Volodya's suicide—nearly a year ago—as well as the confusion and uncertainty over the *Alexander III's* ship committee chairman Vantz's ultimatum. Even though the ultimatum had never borne fruit, she was greatly distressed to learn the so-called commissars had most recently come down to the Black Sea from the Baltic seeking officers to execute.

Roman had many anxious moments, too, when Xenia shared all that had happened to her. It became apparent the no one was left untouched by the wildness of the revolution.

What should he do? In his mind he saw no choice but to return to Sevastopol and the *Alexander III.* He asked Xenia, "Will you accompany me as far as Moscow. From there I can take another train to Sevastopol." They bid goodbye to Roman's family in Torso.

However, there was one thing Roman had to do before leaving

Moscow: he must talk to Nicholas Harvey, asking for his daughter's hand in marriage. Though he stayed at the Harvey home for several days, Roman had difficulty getting to see her father. As editor of one of Moscow's largest newspapers, *Utro Rossii*, 'Russia's Morning', he was always at his office. There was plenty of news...and he was feverishly editing all the stories. Roman gathered courage: he realized he was running out of time; he must go to his office to talk to him.

Xenia's father looked at Roman very suspiciously and when he learned his reason for coming, he just said, "No."

" Why?" Roman asked, astounded.

"You had better wait until the revolution is over...You are too young and the war will probably be over in three or four months." He wanted them to wait. "Then you can be given a proper wedding with all the trimmings."

Roman was shocked. He came back to the house and told Xenia "nothing doing." She, being a very obedient daughter didn't want to go against the wishes of her parents even though she was disappointed. "Well, what can we do?" With sad demeanor, they said their goodbyes.

Roman, feeling he had received a cold shoulder, planned to return to the Black Sea fleet in Sevastopol. At the railroad station, he found the train bulging with people and knew he couldn't get on. However, a navy officer saw him at the station who said, "Hello, what are you doing here?" Roman was told to come into their car. Inside there were twenty hungry sailors from a certain battleship. Roman learned that they were a crew from a ship in the Baltic Sea that had no bread. These sailors, along with one officer, were being sent to the part of Russia where there was still some food and they were to take all they'd gather back to Petrograd.

Roman eventually got back to his ship, safe and sound. He managed to mask his true emotions with a gusty laugh to himself when nothing was done about him being AWOL. But, once inside, he really wasn't laughing.

J & P Oliver

Chapter 16

Roman encountered madness—revolutionary wildness—once he boarded a train back to Sevastopol. Torzhok had been a kind of protected world of peace sheltered from all the worldly bedlam. That illusion was gone. Once again, he was caught up in the confusing welter of conflicting forces. The terrible sense of rejection from her father was swept aside.

Fleetingly, his joyful reunion with Xenia and her affection flashed through his thoughts and with that came the sense of loss.

***

The implications weren't yet distinct, but last November, only a few weeks ago, Russia, driven to her knees, signed an armistice with Germany. The authority for this peace treaty was ostensibly Bolshevik: Lenin and Trotsky were at the nation's helm now. They had surged to power within hours of the revolt which toppled Russia's monarchy for all time. Roman felt surges of anger with all that was happening.

The November armistice had brought no peace: the new revolutionary government introduced only a new kind of violence and the masses of people didn't understand these new contradictory conditions. Millions of soldiers were fleeing, in addition to the thousands of deserters who had already fled the army. The crush of humanity seemed to fill every crevice of the country, roads, streets, trains, and bread lines. Haggard, fright-filled faces on weakened bodies walked to nowhere; a sense of hopelessness permeated everything.

In Sevastopol, Roman's apprehension about his unauthorized leave was unfounded. The desperate situation created by the Bolsheviks had overshadowed all else. In essence, or so it seemed, the armistice actually meant nothing. The Germans desperately needing food, advanced towards the Crimea about to take Nikolayev. The Ukraine and the area near the Crimea was the breadbasket of Russia. Germany's ultimate plan was to take Sevastopol, Russia's major Black Sea naval base. If they captured this base, Germany would pose the gravest of threats to the whole naval fleet. Plus, there were intimations that Russia—that is, Bolshevik Russia—Lenin and Trotsky—were negotiating *something* at a conference in Brest-Litovsk.

Does our nation know anything about what is happening? How can we end this sense of futility? Roman felt the Russian public knew essentially *nothing* of what was actually happening. Rumors floating through society were incomprehensible to anyone other than the negotiators. What did Russia's new Bolshevik government have with which to barter? They were too weak, too disorganized; and there was constant infighting among the Bolsheviks themselves.

Thus, Germany became the ultimate victor in the treaty signed in March 1918 at Brest-Litovsk. Germany gained vast areas in Finland, the Baltic states, Poland and the Ukraine. The Bolsheviks, frustrated and vengeful, resorted to violence.

The aspect of the treaty, which affected Roman most immediately involved the Navy. The Germans wanted the Black Sea Fleet. Fear of capture by the Germans ran so high that even the leaders of the ships' committees of the *Alexander III* and the *Empress Catherine* desperately sought someone to command the fleet's escape. This posed a near unsolvable problem, considering the deteriorating relationship between sailors and officers.

The decision of where to go, however, came quite quickly in the midst of desperation. The only other Black Sea port deep enough to harbor the navy's largest ships was far over on its eastern coast, beyond the Sea of Azov, where the Caucasus Mountains come down to the sea. It was also near Ekaterinodar (later to be named Krasnodar), a long time military town and the administrative center for the region's Cossack army. Ekaterinodar had been the scene of many battles, and the military road passing by its fortress walls was the route over which many revolutionaries had been banished to the Caucasus, including many great writers and poets, like Pushkin, Lermontov and others. The most significant advantage at the moment: it was far removed from the advancing German armies.

They urgently needed an officer with the authority and skills to lead the fleet from Sevastopol to safety. No one was readily available; the mutinous crews supporting the Bolshevik Red forces had usurped command or murdered many of the officers. Negotiations went on for several weeks before Bolshevik leaders realized that the fleet would be needed by whatever government headed Russia. They finally brought Admiral Michael Sablin out of retirement to take command. Sablin was tall, graying man of about fifty, with a reputation for demanding strict obedience to his orders. The ships' committees had trouble considering him but reluctantly accepted him as it seemed there was no other choice.

Sablin was given dictatorial powers as the prime requisite of his acceptance of command.

"All right, I will take the fleet," he told the ships committee leaders. "But only on one condition: that you men take down the red rags flying from our masts and replace them with Russia's St. Andrew's flag. That's the proper identification of the Imperial Russian Navy, in case you have forgotten."

Sablin then added another requirement, even more troublesome to the sailors.

"You men are also to start obeying the officers again, and you must salute them as before. We are no ragtag bunch of mutineers. You are still the Russian Navy!"

The crew heard that General Kornilov had organized a White Army against the Bolsheviks. He had been arrested by Kerensky, but then he escaped to the south and began organizing the army. Many were so angered at Kornilov's arrest that they wanted to join him, but being at sea, they never had a chance.

Sablin remained adamant about his instructions and the committees were in no position to debate the issue. The destiny of the fleet, the bulk of Russia's Black Sea naval forces, was in dire jeopardy. It was learned that the Germans were almost at the outskirts of Sevastopol. Under Sablin's command the St. Andrew's flag reappeared on ships' masts and crews regained their proper attitude towards officers. The return to order, as Sablin made clear, also included morning muster.

Another obstacle in this rising urgency came from a totally unexpected quarter.

Instead of preparing to defend Sevastopol against the encroaching German armies as one would expect townsfolk to do, local leaders—now made up of rebellious sailors and other revolutionaries—led pogroms against the naval officers and the more prosperous townspeople. Rumors were spread that some forty officers were murdered before the town's working men organized to combat the lawless sailors. It was April 1918 before they succeeded in putting an end to the many night thefts and murders.

Despite his dictatorial powers, Adm. Sablin ran into an inescapable problem on issuing one of his very first orders: "The Black Sea fleet is now Ukrainian. By doing this, hopefully we can stave off additional pressure from the Germans. They insist we turn the fleet over to them under the provisions of the Brest-Litovsk Treaty." This order that the fleet was now Ukrainian was so unsatisfactory to most of the crews for that part of the fleet—fourteen destroyers and four supply ships—that they pulled up anchor and left, heading for their destination alone.

Sablin continued negotiating—in vain—for another month about the fate of the rest of the fleet. Finally, on the evening of May 14th, he learned that German patrols had entered the outskirts of Sevastopol. He decided the big ships—and all others able to do so—*had to leave immediately*. In the panic, the officers and crewmen ordered to open the harbor's boom gates disobeyed and ran off. Sablin ordered another team to blow up the remaining ships so that the Germans could not get them, but this team also disappeared. The enemy did manage to capture some of the older ships.

It was necessary to open the harbor's gates for the main bulk of the fleet to escape. Sablin sent several officers and men rushing down to do this; it took time to work the gates open. So, that by the time the two big ships, the *Alexander III* renamed by the Bolsheviks to the *Volya* and the *Catherine the Great* (renamed the *Svobodnaya Rossiia),* were under way, the Germans had overtaken the shore batteries and turned those guns on them. Only the *Volya* got away untouched. Roman became Navigating Officer aboard Sablin's flagship. Other ships, including about a dozen destroyers, increased speed, fleeing harm's way: all too slowly to suit Roman. For him, it was a close shave. Standing near the ship's compass in the lookout position, he had no protection from the ship's 12-inch armor plate as did most of the crew. Shrapnel whistled and ricocheted all about him until they were out of range. Miraculously he wasn't injured.

***

The fleet now found itself under the political authority of one of the new governments that had blossomed in the wake of the revolution, the Kuban-Black Sea Soviet Republic. No one had anticipated this. The group of southern Bolshevik leaders concentrated in this area requested naval help in suppressing some irregular and rebellious Red forces. The fleet personnel persuaded Adm. Sablin to take charge of the new situation.

Sablin's response was to continue with his previous orders, clearly challenging the local Bolsheviks: St. Andrew's flag would fly. He ordered two companies of sailors to restore discipline, and among them were many who would have preferred to kill the Bolsheviks as the simplest way of achieving order. The mere suggestion of such a mass execution resulted in a broad exodus of local communist supporters.

Other pressing matters he deemed even more important to Sablin. Although temporarily safe in Novorossiysk, the fleet was still pursued by Germany. Barely a week after arriving there, he called Roman to his office and showed him a letter he had just received from German Field Marshal Eichorn.

"Sturmer, I need you for special duty," said the Admiral. "It appears we haven't escaped far enough. But we're as far as we can go. No other harbor is deep enough to hold us." He punched a fist into the palm of his other hand. "But this man, this arrogant Eichorn"—he pointed to the letter he had just handed Roman—"This man is now demanding we go back to Sevastopol and turn ourselves over to him, or face the armies coming around from Kerch!"

In his telegram, the German claimed Sablin's flight had been in strict disobedience of the Brest-Litovsk Treaty requiring Russia to turn its entire navy over to Germany—both fleets, the Baltic and the Black Sea, and the small flotilla five thousand miles to the east, in Vladivostok.

Though they had actually agreed to this, the Bolsheviks under Trotsky were now of no mind to do so.

Agitated, Adm. Sablin stormed around the room, "Never! He will never get our ships!" Abruptly he stopped and turned to Roman. "Sturmer, I want you go up into the hills north of us and watch what the Germans do. They'll blockade us, I'm sure. I must know the size of their fleet. Stay there and watch for any activity—on land, also. They're near Kerch. But Germany will make sure we can go nowhere else," Admiral Sablin's voice rose angrily as he pounded his desk.

"I will deny any breach of the Treaty and try for some kind of negotiations. I don't expect any success, but Eichorn is able to bottle us up here. Take six men," he ordered, "and find a good spot in the hills where you can keep an eye on the Germans' movement, on the water and towards the Crimea...whatever you can see. And keep an eye open for submarines."

"Yes, sir," replied Roman as he left the Admiral's office. What he didn't know was that Adm. Sablin faced an even greater dilemma.

***

The telegram from Field Marshal Eichorn had not been the only thing distressing Sablin, and after dismissing Roman, he began wrestling with a kind of dilemma he had never encountered before in his entire naval career. It was caused not by German Field Marshal Eichorn but by Sablin's own superior commanders. Lenin himself had sent Sablin secret orders informing him he might soon receive a message, clear and not encoded, ordering him to hand over his fleet to the Germans. This was puzzling enough, and directly contrary to Sablin's own wisdom. *Give Russia's Black Sea fleet to the enemy? Never!* Everything in his own soul ordered Sablin to keep the fleet out of German hands or die in the attempt. The fleet was a symbol of what he had spent a lifetime defending. It represented Russia, or at least disappearing elements of it.

But in the next breath, Lenin instructed him that if he did receive such a message in the clear, it was really a signal that *he was to sink his ships at once!*

The decision: either obey Eichorn and hand the fleet over to the Germans, or, under orders of Lenin, sink all the ships. Either way Sablin would become the person who destroyed the Russian Black Sea navy. He had been around long enough to understand the political ramifications of military strategies. If he, Sablin handed over Russia's fleet, it would give the Germans new sufficient strength at sea which could change the balance of the Great War from the Allies to Germany and Austria. He could in no honorable way do that—even though Germany had legitimate authority under the Brest-Litovsk Treaty. How can I disregard Lenin's orders? Sablin knew he had to go to Moscow in an attempt to negotiate a different kind of strategy.

Chapter 17

In the cool of a May 1918 morning, Roman and his six hand-picked crew members traipsed the twenty-or-so miles from the Novorossiysk harbor over the ridge into the northern hills above the harbor to follow Sablin's orders. They walked at an easy, steady pace. Their destination was a small lookout cabin on a point located northwest of the bay above the Black Sea. In direct contrast to the ever-present sounds of war, the hills were peacefully quiet except for the sounds of nature and a few conversations. It was tempting to sit down and relax in the tranquil setting.

Roman, however, always remaining on alert, did not allow the band of men to become complacent. He led the group carrying weapons and necessary equipment including a wireless. "I don't know what we'll find, so keep a sharp look out all around you," he ordered. "The lookout cabin will be our main area from which we will report any noticeable activity on the water. However—we will also watch out for *any* activity in this area. We'll take shifts of being on patrol."

The vantage point allowed Roman and his crew to serve as spotters for their ship's big guns. Their coded communication allowed their ship to lob shells over the ridge and hit surfaced German U-boats whenever they were alerted by Roman's group. Although the transmissions were risky, the naval codes at that time were considered fairly secure.

Roman became a little bored as time passed slowly. There wasn't much to do except keep continual watch on the bay, sighting enemy ships, and enjoying the surrounding beauty, climate, and charm of this famous North Caucasus region of the Black Sea. Known for its picturesque views, fresh air, southern sun, mild climate and fertile grounds, the area was part of the historical Ekaterinodar (Krasnodar 1920) region known since ancient times for its vineyards and wines, especially champagne. The area was rich in the history of being inhabited by different nations and multiple battles. Roman found himself wondering about some of the battles as well as the vineyards.

One day on a patrol, Roman and the team arrived at the famous Lake Abrau framed by mountains and relic forests. It was several miles from their lookout point and to their delight they were greeted by cold springs, mountain streams, and rivulets rushing down the slopes to and from the lake. Lake Abrau was the biggest lake in the Black Sea region.

Roman knew about the legend of the lake and told it to the crew who were unfamiliar with it.

The Ancient Legend of the Lake

There was once a poor shepherd named Durso who fell in love with Abrau, a rich man's beautiful daughter. But the girl's parents forbade her to see the youth. One time, the rich man hosted an outdoor feast and the guests amused themselves by throwing flat cakes around them, like disks, in front of the poor hungry villagers. Allah was not pleased and punished them by opening up the earth so that the entire village and its inhabitants disappeared into the abyss.

It so happened that Abrau was visiting her beloved and on the way home, the absence of any signs of the village shocked her so that she jumped from a cliff into the water. However, she did not drown because the lake refused to engulf her. She ran over the water surface and joined her beloved on the other side of the lake. Since that time, on a clear night, under a silvery moon, one can see the traces of the lovely maiden when she appears on the water.

The Abrau Valley, as it was known ("abrau" meaning precipice or bluff), was rich with vineyards and cool waters from the River Abrau that meandered its way down to the Black Sea. The magnificence was staggering to the imagination of the group. They found the beautiful lake surrounded by lush greenery and filled with numerous fish. The quietness made war seem far away. To some, it seemed that the Creator of the World had been very generous with His paintbrush in this region.

Roman was the first to find that north of the lookout cabin, in the valley, was a big estate called Abrau-Durso, created in 1870 by the government of Czar Alexander II for the purpose of vine growing and wine-making. From then on, Abrau-Durso had been the primary producer of traditional wine. In 1890-95 underground champagne-storage tunnels were built and until 1917 when French specialists worked there making the award-winning champagne left, their secrets were never revealed to the Russians. It wasn't until after 1920 that the Russians discovered them. Happy was the day Roman discovered the vineyard.

Covering close to 1500 acres, the vineyard was nearly abandoned. Much of the beauty was destroyed or marred, having been overrun by looting Bolsheviks and other roving bands who were no longer in evidence. Only a few guards remained, caretakers really, who knew little of what was going on outside the estate walls. Glad to see a new face, one scraggly caretaker took Roman through the castle—and to Roman's astonishment and delight—showed him the wine cellar.

Roman couldn't believe his eyes! There were stacked, rack after rack, in long, seemingly endless corridors, bottle upon bottle of champagne! *There must be a million bottles of champagne still stored here!* After the tour, Roman chatted with the guard at length. He thanked the guard profusely when he gave him a keg of white wine. He was even more overjoyed when the guard invited him back.

East of Abrau-Durso winery, Roman also discovered an estate of a wealthy man, the writer and critic Mikhail Katkov. His country home was beautiful, but sadly, it had also been looted and the family driven off by the revolutionaries. The huge, magnificent library was ransacked. Books were thrown helter-skelter into huge piles onto the now dusty floor; many torn. Once poor and desperate peasants had torn out the fine onion skin pages in some of the rare volumes to use for cigarette paper. Paper, like food, had become scarce. The prominent estate that had grown grapes for the Abrau winery now lay abandoned by the family. This sacrilege of the home and the library tore at Roman.

Here, too, one old man was left behind as caretaker. "Would it be all right if I took some books to read?" Roman asked. To his delight, the response was, "Yes."

Back at the lookout cabin, Roman asked the sailors to make shelves behind his bed for the books and then he fixed a spot for the keg of white wine he'd gotten from the winery. He attached a hose to the keg and put this in his mouth. Then he read and sipped to his heart's content when off duty. When the keg was empty, he simply replenished it by going back and talking to the guard at the winery. *This is wonderful* went through Roman's mind many times.

Chapter 18

A doctrine of terror cloaked Russia in 1918. Lenin in dictatorship-like manner evoked military expeditions into the countryside and the Volga region to seize food from the peasants. He censored newspapers and sent secret police to spy on them. Some hostages were taken to prisons and others were shot. Russia continued to fall apart and people wondered how did all this happen?

In contrast, Roman's life as a lookout at the winery was extremely pleasant. The idyllic life continued through June and July, but his situation changed in just one evening when he received a short call from a friend on the *Emperor Alexander III*.

"Hello...do you want to go to Moscow?"

"Sure," replied Roman quickly. He thought he might have a chance to see Xenia. He'd written several times since being with her at the reunion in January, but he had no idea if she had received any of his letters: there had been no word from her since the reunion which worried him. Getting mail through, by any means, was as difficult as everything else in their incredibly confused world.

"Well, come back to the ship right away," his friend ordered. "Admiral Sablin wants you." He gave no details and Roman needed none. If ordered, he would go.

He lost no time in leaving his cabin—books, wine and all. Hurriedly packing his meager belongings and leaving another man behind in charge of the observation detachment, Roman and one of his crewmen began walking along the trail over the ridge back to Novorossiysk, some twenty miles distant.

They walked all night in order to make it in time for whatever Roman's friend had in mind for the upcoming Moscow trip. Weary and red-eyed from lack of sleep and footsore from the hike, the two reached the *Emperor Alexander III* just as the sun came up. As they approached the pier, however, they could see that something wasn't quite right. Roman was immediately on guard. *Is this a trap?* The ship was there but there was no gangplank, not even a ladder between the ship and the pier, only a narrow plank with several ladders hanging to the water's edge. Roman didn't allow himself to get frightened.

"Halloo, ship! " Roman hailed. The only response was from several crewmen looking down on him and his crew member.

"Why is there no boarding ladder?" yelled Roman.

"Those are our orders!" a sailor called back, pointing to the narrow plank between the pier and ship. "That's to discourage us from coming back to the ship too drunk to walk that. If we can't stay sober enough to navigate it, we have to suffer the consequences. Think you can make it?" The sailors at the ship's rail guffawed.

In spite of his weariness, Roman mentally heaved a sigh of relief and walked the plank safely. Behind him the other sailor teetered a bit, but also managed without toppling into the water. Even sober, it was no easy task.

As they came aboard ship, Roman stopped. He was was shocked. Stacked against the walls of the officers' wardroom were case after case of champagne from Abrau-Durso Winery! "I don't believe this! I only chose one keg of white wine and look what the officers took...all that champagne," he muttered to himself. He spent quite a while chiding himself, but finally made peace by remembering that, wine or champagne, he had thoroughly enjoyed life in that tiny cabin, sipping through his straw and reading to his heart's content. He could not have asked for finer duty.

***

The purpose of the trip to Moscow was in no way designed for Roman's benefit even though he looked at it as a chance to see Xenia once again: that was Roman's *own* interpretation—an opportunity superimposed strictly by himself on military strategy.

When he reported to Admiral Sablin, he was shocked to learn of the admiral's dilemma over Field Marshal Eichorn's demands, as well as the secret message from Lenin.

Sablin briefed Roman of his plans to try to work out a different strategy with Lenin and Trotsky, now commander in chief of the army. "I must go to Moscow to talk to this man Trotsky," he told Roman. "I want you to accompany me to be in charge of my bodyguards. Quickly, choose thirty men to prepare to come with us. We'll leave as soon as possible."

Sablin was given two railway cars and a locomotive to hold him and his contingent, but it took longer than expected to actually obtain that equipment. Considering the total disorganization of transportation facilities, they were fortunate to get anything at all. At first there was neither engineer nor firemen to operate the locomotive set aside for Sablin. Trains only ran haphazardly: there were no schedules. In some places, lines were ripped up by either Red or White forces—depending on which held that particular area at the moment. Finally, an engineer and a fireman were persuaded to take Sablin's train to Moscow, taking along the flour to trade for clothes when they got there.

Thousands of bedraggled people were going in every direction, aimlessly, it seemed. They were either fleeing one army or the other, rioting, or standing futilely in some bread line.

In the midst of all the delays, still another unexpected situation arose. The Admiral rode in the first railroad car with two aides, Lt. Roman Levgovd as his senior aide, and Anatole Goursky as the junior office. From time to time Roman received a briefing there. Twenty-five men in Roman's charge were in the second car. The Admiral's group soon found itself in strange company. At the last minute a third car was added to the train, carrying the commander-in-chief of the Red troops fighting General Kornilov's White forces. It was necessary for the railroad to take the General or he would cause trouble. This General was a veterinarian, and only an intern at that. Yet, he was in charge of the Red troops.

Tension was felt everywhere.

Unknown to Sablin at the time, an emissary from Trotsky was en route from Moscow to Novorossiysk, who could cause great damage to the Black Sea fleet. This commissar was a Russian naval officer from another academy who went by the name of Raskolnikoff. He had become a Bolshevik, but in changing loyalties that would later bring about his liquidation: but not in time to prevent great damage.

Roman was ignorant of all this maneuvering as the train worked its way to Moscow. Since the car in which Adm. Sablin rode was immediately behind the locomotive and the coal car, a restless Roman persuaded the engineer and fireman to let him ride up with them. Ever inquisitive, he'd always wanted to learn the ins and outs of operating such a massive machine. The slowness of the trip enabled him to have sufficient lessons to handle the very basics of train operation.

In Moscow, the entourage was met by some naval officers who gave warm greetings accompanied by grave warnings. "You have to get out of Moscow immediately! You'll be captured on sight!" The officers gave Sablin no details, only that he was in immediate danger.

Plans to escape were hastily made, but what could such a large contingent do to make themselves invisible? The best thing would be to split up and somehow individually work their way to a specific safe area. All but Roman agreed. He explained to the Admiral about his fiancée, Xenia. "I have to find her," he said. "I've had not heard from her in more than six months." Adm. Sablin was understanding and let him go. "But, only for the one night."

The friendly officers would be able to hide Sablin and his bodyguard, but then, they must quickly leave the city. Roman was told where the contingent would be secreted and instructed to be back the next day. It was *imperative* that Sablin's whole group get back to the fleet in Novorossiysk as quickly as possible. The engineer and fireman of their train were optimistic that they could get some additional fuel and be ready for a return by the next day.

Roman's small sack of flour for Xenia was brought on the basis of all that he had heard about people starving in Moscow. It was not much, but hopefully anything would help. It was all he had. Since her father held a key position as editor of the Morning of Russia newspaper, Roman hoped the Harvey family would be at least somewhat better off than most of the people.

Xenia was at home and, overjoyed, ran to Roman giving him a big hug. She expressed appreciation for the flour and quickly answered some of his questions.

She reassured Roman, "Things are not well with us here in Moscow, but we are surviving. We have a lot to share. There are still a few restaurants where we can go and have a brief time together." They took their time walking in the warm weather and talking.

During their meager meal, they made the most of their stolen moments trying to memorize each other's face and ignore the turmoil around them. While they held hands, Xenia told him how bad things were. Her details were worse than the rumors he had heard. To add to Roman's dismay, Xenia told him, "Father still won't change his mind about our marrying. 'No,' he said, just as he did months ago, 'this is not a good time. Wait till the revolution is over,' he advised me sternly. I can't make him see how much I want to get married."

Roman put his arm around Xenia's shoulders as her eyelashes glistened with tears. Then he asked, "Does he really believe there is an end to this senseless war, or does he just not want you to marry me?"

"I don't know. Father must realize by now that this revolution is not just a brief disruption. He knows the Bolsheviks are a grave threat to our Russian way of life: but he seems to keep that opinion to himself; he tries not to be too controversial in the newspaper."

Parting the next day was the hardest Roman and Xenia had ever experienced. It was almost unbearable for Xenia as she kissed Roman a teary goodbye. Ominous shadows loomed over their parting, considering how conditions were deteriorating. Xenia feared for Roman's life and couldn't even guess when they would see each other again. The Bolsheviks had put terror in the air with their strict measures. Horror stories of people being jailed and tortured increased daily.

Roman and Xenia hugged tightly for a long last moment. Then Xenia looked at him, still trying to memorize his features. She saw a thin Roman with the same hair and facial features, but with a look of sadness in his eyes. Turning, she ran out of sight, unable to prolong her tears and their departure any longer. She felt she would never see him again.

Chapter 19

Roman faced a complete mystery when he reached the pre-arranged meeting point at the train. Sablin and his aides were nowhere to be seen. Nor were the bodyguards anywhere. Stunned, Roman cautiously looked around the train station to see if anyone might be following him and then returned to the train. The engineer and fireman were there impatient to return, anxious to be away from Moscow before someone suddenly demanded use of their train. They had made their trades of flour and supplies for clothing and urgently wanted to be on their way back.

Suddenly Roman was spotted by Lt. Levgovd stepping out of one of the three cars. "Sturmer!" he called, hurrying toward his friend.

"What has happened?" asked Roman, "Where is everyone... the Admiral, the men?"

Levgovd hunched his shoulders. "I don't know. Just gone."

"But ...," Roman started, then abruptly stopped as he saw a small group of his men hurriedly dismounting from the train.

Levgovd put his hand on Roman's arm. "That's all that's left of your men. The other twenty have disappeared."

Roman stared at Levgovd questioningly. Levgovd replied, "That's all I know, my friend. We were waiting, when suddenly the Admiral came back. He hurriedly said he was leaving. When I started asking questions, he said he had no time, and wouldn't tell me if he did. He was being sought by Bolsheviks and was taking Lt. Goursky with him. He asked me to stay, to explain to you, and then said we should leave Moscow as quickly as possible. That's all he told me—nothing more—except to tell the bodyguards they were free to go. They were free to go wherever they wanted—wherever they could find safety. It seems

125

the Bolsheviks have orders to capture and execute all of us before any questions can be asked of them."

Upon hearing this news, Roman's stomach clenched even more. He felt ill. Once again, his life was at stake because of the insanity surrounding them. He had a quick flashback to the deadly situation when Herbert Vantz had calmly said they were executing everyone with German names aboard ship.

"So, they've all gone," Levgovd was saying as Roman forced his mind back to the present. "I don't know where. The Admiral gave me no hint. 'Too dangerous', he said." Levgovd continued, "The fewer people who knew, the better. These five," he said turning to the men who had grouped together just out of earshot of the two officers, waiting uncertainly, looking around nervously every moment or so. "These five chose to stay with me." Levgovd took a deep breath and shrugged as he finished. "What else is there to say?"

For a moment Roman was too stunned to ask anything. It was too late anyway. So, he made a decision and simply said, "Let's get back on the train. I'll tell the trainmen to pull out." He motioned for the crewmen to climb into the train again, smiling to let them know he was glad to see them again, and then joined Levgovd as the train began to crawl away.

"Keep out of sight," Levgovd urged. "If the cars appear empty maybe no one will pay attention." So they hunkered down and sat on the floor away from the windows as the train moved slowly out of Moscow and gradually gained speed.

Roman never saw Admiral Sablin or Lt. Goursky again.

The engineer and fireman found themselves in a more difficult situation traveling south than on the northbound trip. The direct rail lines from Moscow that had been open on the trip north were now damaged or broken from bombings or simply torn up and the rails hauled away. They got only as far as Blastoff because the track was out. Russia was a country in the midst of chaos and severe warfare—worse than before—from both the Red and White armies. The trainmen fervently struggled to keep the train moving, back-tracking when necessary, switching when possible, wending their way east, snakelike.

Finally, one of the lines they chose led them a great distance out of their way and eventually ended abruptly at Kamyshin, a town of goodly size on the edge of the Volga River once noted for its watermelon trade.

The river was a scene of much frenetic activity due to the rail line stopping there. During normal times, goods and people could be changed quickly from train to ship with a minimum of trouble. Now, because the railroads were in such shambles, people pushed, shoved, and crowded in desperation onto the ships that still worked their way up and down the Volga.

Polite consideration no longer existed.

The continual threat of capture and the disappearance of Adm. Sablin and their original entourage in Moscow rested heavily with both Roman and Lt. Levgovd. They constantly surveyed the crowds trying to be inconspicuous, hoping no one would cause them new troubles. As it turned out, their group of two naval officers, two trainmen, and five sailors, caused hardly more than a glance from the throngs as they moved between the railroad station and the piers where several ships were tied up.

After some cautious questioning of stevedores at the pier, Levgovd took the lead to a ship headed downriver. It seemed to be their best option—and perhaps their only one. He said, "We can then get a train straight to Novorossiysk if we get off at Tzaritzin."

Spirits revived, especially when Roman mentioned he had an uncle in Tzaritzin who had been a colonel in the Czarist army. The area had a long history of military action and several times the city had changed sides during the Civil War.

Roman led them to his uncle's home, but to Roman's dismay, the uncle became an obstacle: he tried to dissuade Roman from returning to his ship in Novorossiysk. "It would be much better to join Trotsky and Lenin." The situation seemed even worse when they learned that now Tzaritzin was the headquarters of the Red Army in the region!

"Roman, my boy," repeated his uncle, "be sensible. There is no Czar any more, no monarchy. Times have changed. This is a proletariat world now. Lots of officers, army, and navy like you, have changed their minds to keep up with this changing world. Hear me, Roman! Be wise."

"I don't care. I do not like them."

"Them? Who are them? Them—they are all of us, common people, everybody. . . everybody but the wealthy, and the stubborn, like you."

"No, Uncle," Roman said, trying to appear calm as he recognized how this talk was drifting into dangerous waters, "We will go on. We must stand up for what we feel is right. We are under orders, as you are. We will respect yours, and I hope you will respect ours. After all, sir, we are family, isn't that so?" He kept his voice mild, despite the anger rising within him.

Fortunately his uncle smiled, clapped him on the back and said heartily, "Of course, my boy. Family is everything. Without family what is left? Have a safe trip, all of you." He grabbed Roman in a traditional hug and let him go with a wide, gap-toothed smile that had none of the warmth and friendliness his words were supposed to portray.

Roman and his uncle quickly parted ways. Once they were safely away from his uncle's home, Roman voiced his fears. "We need to leave. Now. My uncle is very different from the man I knew in my childhood. Keep your eyes and ears open," he told Levgovd, "I do not trust him. If he can switch from loyalty to the Czar to loyalty to the Bolsheviks, why should I trust him not to order his own troops to capture us? We'd better pray the train leaves quickly."

***

This is too much, Roman thought as he stared from the Novorossiysk's pier out to the empty harbor before him. *Where have the ships gone? Have the Germans overpowered the crews and simply taken them to sea?* He dismissed that thought almost instantly, because the German soldiers— supposedly not sailors—were drawing closer. *Surely the soldiers won't know how to navigate a ship as big as Alexander, Admiral Sablin's flagship. Or, have the Germans managed to force the ships' crews into going to sea? Or, ...is it conceivable that Sablin himself has somehow managed to come back here and steal them? Or… have they been discovered by the Germans and forced to take the ships to sea?* Roman had no way of answering his own questions.

Some people—looking like bedraggled sailors—came down the pier coming toward them. He and Levgovd had only arrived at the pier-side railroad tracks just a few minutes ago. Everyone of the group just stood there, as puzzled as Roman. *Hopefully these people know something.*

As Roman looked back at the harbor, he saw something which sent chills through him. The newcomers confirmed Roman's suspicions when he confronted them. "Your people sank half the ships, then pulled anchor and sailed away." They just shrugged and told him what they knew.

Roman found out that on June 18th, the *Svobodnaya Rossiia* was torpedoed and sunk by the destroyer *Kerch* in order to prevent it from falling into German hands. He was outraged and clenched his teeth in order not to say something he'd regret. *Why would they do a thing like that?* He could not take his eyes off the sight, now that he realized what he was seeing. Tips of the superstructure of some of the ships showed above the waves. The destroyers told the story. *That's our ship's funnels, our signal masts that I can barely see above the water's surface. Where have the others gone?*

"I heard someone say," claimed one of the men who had just arrived, "that they were going to Sevastopol. That they would be safer there than here."

Sevastopol? Admiral Sablin brought the fleet here to be safe from the Germans advancing on Sevastopol, and now we're being told that the Emperor Alexander III and whatever remained of the fleet is back there… impossible. Yet… all my belongings are in Sevastopol, too. That means another unexpected side trip.

This reversal overwhelmed Roman. Nothing was where it was supposed to be any more. A rush of weakness and dizziness weakened Roman to the point that he put out his arm and grasped Levgovd's shoulder. His friend looked at him.

"Roman, what—are you all right?"

"Yes, yes. Fine." He shook his head, smiled weakly and

straightened his shoulders to show he was all right. But, inwardly he was not all right. He shouldn't be on this pier in Novorossiysk, looking at an empty harbor broken only by the shattered remains of *his* navy poking out of the water!

Images flitted through Roman's mind of all that had happened to him in the last two years. They came at him as a sudden rush of disastrous scenes and events. Without warning, discouragement enveloped him. The last two years of his life were actually the first two years of his career as an officer in the Imperial Russian Navy, a thing which no longer existed—at least officially. *There is no Imperial Russia. Anything so named is now the enemy. Is this what the people want? And, here I am in the midst of a war, on the run, considered a traitor by whatever could be called the government.*

Unable to fight, Roman felt despair. He was at a loss—actually humiliated—by the quickly shifting strategies that didn't last long enough to be implemented. His present recollection about serving the Imperial Russian Navy was unbelievable. He was a man under suspicion, under threat of execution, a man in hiding—or fleeing first one authority then another. He had to keep looking over his shoulder for commissars who were out murdering naval officers like himself. Adm. Sablin had declared, "Madness!" They were supposed to save the fleet, escape from Sevastopol to here, and now *here* the ships rested in pieces, destroyed, scuttled as one set of orders had demanded. The other ships, in obedience to other orders, were God knows where—maybe back at Sevastopol. And here he stood.

Roman, Levgovd, and five other men—the remnants of the Black Sea fleet—were in fact stripped of their equipment and weapons. *How humiliating,* Roman thought to himself. *How ironic. This is nothing like the glorious career I envisioned those years ago when I first set foot in the Admiralty in St. Petersburg, so excited to begin my naval career.* He continued to mourn. He now faced a future that was as bleak as a becalmed sea, placid, deceitful. He finally turned to Levgovd. "So. We return to Sevastopol," he said with little inflection.

Levgovd nodded, "It's the only home we have."

Chapter 20

"You're right, Levgovd," Roman replied more to himself than to his friend. "We're all homeless." *Homeless.* It hit him in the pit of his stomach. He'd known fear, but it was nothing like this. Nothing to look forward to and nothing to dream about.

"What are we to do?" Levgovd quietly responded.

"Sevastopol is the only place that can remotely be called a home base, but there's no lodging there. Nothing. We'd better find some place here to hide....and quickly."

Finding no other solution, they hid temporarily in an empty railroad car at the edge of the Novorossiysk pier hoping they could eventually find a way to Sevastopol. It was hot and dirty. Smelly. The situation gave them no end of trouble.

"There're bugs crawling over me," Roman yelped! "This is intolerable. I can't sleep! I feel like I have bugs everywhere."

"Me, too!" Levgovd was quick to agree as he scratched at his legs. "Let's chance sleeping in the railroad station. There was a restaurant near the railroad station that used to serve excellent food."

Roman thought that the unexpected treat beckoned—in spite of the danger. "Hopefully, it's still there."

"Let's hope. I remember their Borscht and cutlets...Their cutlets were something like hamburger, ground meat...but the patties were thick, with good gravy," Levgovd said.

Fortunately, no one accosted them on their way. To their relief, they found the restaurant open. Briefly, they looked behind them first and then into the restaurant. It was almost empty and seemed to be void of any seamen. Quickly and quietly they ate keeping their heads down, slurping their food as if they had no etiquette. After their meal, walking low, they safely returned to their hideout.

For several days the pair stayed put, even as boredom increased along with their apprehension of possibly being discovered by Red forces. Novorossiysk now teemed with dirty, unkempt, armed men, making it difficult to identify them as Red or White soldiers. They took turns furtively scouting the area and trying to glean information.

One day, Roman Levgovd, whom Roman called his "namesake," made an attempt to alleviate the boredom. "Sturmer, let's organize a republic."

At first Roman laughed at the idea, but quickly became serious and humored his friend. "All right, but which one?" He could continue the joke as well as Levgovd.

"Gelendjik," Levgovd replied quickly. Gelendjik was a tiny area not far from Novorossiysk, southward on the Black Sea which had potential for being a popular resort. But, now, in late summer 1918, there were no authorities and nothing but a clump of huts. It seemed forlorn like everything else.

"OK," Roman continued, joking. He was feeling some relief at the lightheartedness of the game. "You be president. What'll I be?"

"You can be in charge of all communications."

Roman realized suddenly that his "namesake" was not joking. Levgovd went on, "I have already gone to Ekaterinburg and have confirmation from the Red authority that I can organize a new republic!"

"When did you do that?"

Levgovd answered, "The other day when I was out scouting. I listened to conversations and pretended I was Red." Apparently what had sparked Levgovd's imagination were two unoccupied automobiles he'd spied in Gelendjik at some kind of coast guard point. "One vehicle is a Mercedes, the other a French make of some kind," he informed Roman who didn't care. After all, an automobile was transportation, wasn't it? A way to carry them out of Novorossiysk?

"I will use those, since I am President," Levgovd said with the voice of authority.

"With the Reds' permission to travel in hand, and with great caution and much good luck, we can make it safely to Sevastopol."

Roman wasted no time in joining this "new republic". Armed with "authority", he and Levgovd descended upon Gelendjik and commandeered the two cars. They even enlisted a chauffeur to drive one of them away from the site and to teach Roman how to drive. He could navigate a ship, but he'd never learned to drive until now when he was given the basics. One day, while he was behind the wheel of the French car, and Levgovd the Mercedes, they all went to visit the chauffeur's family on the Taman Peninsula, at the edge of Gelendjik. In route, a flock of geese waddling along were suddenly in the middle of the road. The inexperienced Roman panicked, forgetting how to brake. Unable to avoid them, he plowed right through them.

"Stop!" the chauffeur yelled over the raucous cries of the birds. Roman finally managed to bring the car to an abrupt stop. Quickly, he jumped out of the car and grabbed two geese that hadn't escaped. Later at the chauffeur's home, with the family, they enjoyed the two geese along with a huge omelet.

Roman complemented the impromptu hostess. "I shall never forget this meal. It was wonderful. Thank you."

Then they departed the chauffeur and his family and returned to the pier in the Mercedes.

That was the end of the "new republic" and the French automobile.

***

For several days, a whole new world was opened for the two "thieves" because of the Mercedes. Getting gasoline for it was a problem, but they soon found some to steal. Roman watched while Levgovd poured. Finally, they went back to the region where they'd been staying.

One day while driving around practicing his driving skills by himself, Roman got confused and was uncertain how to find his way back to the Novorossiysk pier and Levgovd. Looking around for help, he recognized another friend from Sevastopol walking down the road.

"Jitkoff!" he called. "What are you doing here?"

The man ran to the car. "Sturmer! This is a surprise. I ask you, what are you doing way over here in Novorossiysk?"

Roman excitedly shared their long story with Lt. Jitkoff and then asked him the way back to the pier. "And now, Levgovd and I are trying to get back to Sevastopol. Can you help us?" He was becoming more and more nervous about getting back to the ship and his belongings.

However, Jitkoff rattled off a long tale of his own. "I've fallen in love with a girl in town, Katavanna, whose father doesn't want her to marry me. I've come back to steal her away," he said eying Sturmer mischievously. "Will you help me?"

"Yes," Roman replied with some hesitation, " I will help you find a way…but how about you helping me first?"

"Sure, you bet!" Jitkoff unhesitatingly answered. "That should be easy enough. Let's go find Levgovd."

They reached the pier and left the car while they searched the pier on foot. They couldn't find Levgovd or the Mercedes—to their chagrin it was gone. However, Roman had been able to collect his meager belongings he'd had at the pier. Now, getting away from the main area of Novorossiysk proved harder than they expected.

They learned that everyone in town was required to have a permit from the town's Commandant. They suspected he was probably a Red officer which gave them great misgivings. It was doubtful their plan would work; they'd probably be arrested the moment they showed their hand. No one accosted them all during the time they were planning. Fortunately, they found out that the Commandant wasn't a Red.

When the pair bravely marched into the Commandant's office and talked to his secretary, she promised to give them a permit right away.

All they needed to get to Sevastopol was a boat and to first arrange for it to take them from Novorossiysk to Kerch, a little town across from the Taman peninsula at the southern edge of the Sea of Azov. This town and Taman formed a narrow strait leading northward out of the Black Sea. With Jitkoff's help, Roman succeeded in locating a Greek smuggler who hauled contraband to Kerch. They worked out a deal with him as an escape route.

Jitkoff's personal plan was less complicated, but required considerable finesse on Roman's part. Roman went along with it since he didn't know what had happened to Levgovd and the car.

"Here's what," Jitkoff said. "You talk to Katavanna's old man and keep him busy while I go around to the back of the house and help her out the window. I'll take her right to the pier. After about twenty minutes you can leave her father and meet us at the pier."

The plan worked like a charm. Roman was introduced to the girl's father and kept him busy in conversation for the allotted time, talking about the warm August weather and various events happening in 1918. Then he bid the father goodbye and rushed to meet the two elopers aboard the smuggler's boat going to Kerch. In actuality, they were now part of the contraband being smuggled out of Novorossiysk along with a lot of other people.

There were so many people on deck that the boat nearly capsized before it got away from shore: everyone was afraid of going below. There was no other choice, so Roman and some others went below with the contraband to help stabilize the vessel.

They never reached Kerch.

The smuggler's boat was intercepted by another boat whose captain ordered them to go to Taman, to see the President. No one knew anything about him—who he was or what he was—but they learned that Taman was predominantly White, under the rule of the Cossacks. These Cossacks hated sailors because so many had joined the Red army after the ships had been scuttled. Roman and Jitkoff were overjoyed, because if this were the case, there was no way the presidential rule in Taman was Red.

"Who are you?" asked the President when they were brought before him.

Lt. Jitkoff said he was the commander of a destroyer.

"I'm Lieutenant Sturmer. I was the navigator of the battleship of the Russian Black Sea fleet," Roman declared proudly.

"How do I know that you're not ordinary sailors?" the President asked eyeing their attire and condition. "Show me your hands." He was searching for calluses that would indicate sailors' hard work. He found none.

"Let me see your arms," he persisted.

They showed him, and he leaned forward as he saw the tattoo on Roman's left forearm of a Japanese dragon breathing smoke and lightning, and one on Jitkoff's left hand of an anchor.

"Aha! And you try to tell me you're not sailors."

While sailors made a habit of getting tattooed, officers had been forbidden. The very act of forbidding them had made these officers go ahead and get tattooed. The President was persistent to the point of interrogating Jitkoff and Roman as though they were prisoners. He didn't believe their answers to his questions. He carried his suspicions as far as asking them to tell him what paintings hung in the corridor outside the main mess hall at the naval academy in Petrograd. In turn, they vainly tried to place him among any of their classmates of 1915.

"Where did you come from?" they dared to ask. "Why are you asking questions that seem totally irrelevant? What do you have against sailors?"

"You are right. I don't like sailors. I was expelled from the naval academy in 1908," he confessed. Eventually, however, the President accepted their answers and let them go back to their boat where Katavanna was waiting.

But where were their belongings now? They had all been stolen from the boat. Angrily, they stormed back to the President and accused him of having someone steal them.

"Preposterous!" he exclaimed. "Impossible!"

The two insisted. Finally the President called one of his assistants. Upon learning that the accusation was true, he called his men and let loose with his anger.

Jitkoff and Roman finally got their belongings and Katavanna—a a dark-haired and beautiful Georgian—and themselves to Kerch. From there they took a ship that still made regular trips to Sevastopol. Aboard ship, they had a big party to celebrate the kidnapping and impending marriage. At last in Sevastopol, they stopped at several restaurants to continue the celebration. They were a happy bunch of abductors.

The marriage took place one day later, but to Roman's surprise, they didn't even invite him to the wedding! They totally ignored all that he'd gone through for them! He'd not only acted as a decoy with Katavanna's father, but had gone through the subsequent ordeal with the President of Kerch.

Roman was offended, but his dismay at being excluded quickly disappeared. He was in Sevastopol, just where he thought he wanted to be. That was the end of the "new republic" scheme. . . and Jitkoff.

J & P Oliver

Chapter 21

Things were frighteningly different in Sevastopol. His ship was under German flag. With German sentries all around, permission was required to get to his cabin in order to get his belongings. He obtained permission and hastily grabbed his things, saw the purser and managed to get paid his salary—money that wasn't worth much. He thanked the Lord he wasn't taken prisoner and hastily left the ship.

Leaving, Roman kept to the background, sensing he could be accosted at any moment. A remnant of German forces or some self-appointed Bolshevik enforcers could single him out—another officer to murder. Although squads were fewer there now than in the beginning, they had reappeared with an ominous regularity ever since Lenin and Trotsky had toppled the monarchy in 1917. But the war against the Germans had changed things again. Last March the Brest-Litovsk Treaty had ostensibly ended that war for Russia, giving Germany far too much of the spoils. Most people didn't care; they were just glad to be out of the war. Of course there was not much to be glad about.

Now in September, war and starvation were everywhere. People searched frantically for food and shelter at the first frightening signs of winter: they wandered and hunted. They traded their few remaining belongings; thieved; lied; and did whatever gave them some shred of comfort or some piece of promise.

Money was worthless. It couldn't even buy food or warmth.

Roman was now a civilian, barely surviving. He found several old crew members and with their help he found an abandoned apartment in which to live. The whole area seemed as lifeless as Roman felt. *Some of my former shipmates are busy doing something. What can I do?*

Increasingly, over the past many months, Roman had experienced fears arising from being a naval officer. His life was always in jeopardy. And thus, he could be a target for this revolutionary group or that. But life ashore was depressing and he spent much time alone away from friends and family. He felt like he'd failed and didn't want them to know—especially Xenia. He'd lost contact with her although he thought of her all the time.

Roman realized that thousands of other officers and sailors, still loyal to the old order, suffered the same as he. He needed to do something about it. He always seemed to be on the run from some authority or other, legitimate or fake. The only way he felt he could maintain some form of stability was to take a stronger stand against the Bolsheviks. Bolshevism under Lenin and Trotsky had not brought order to Russia: chaos and terror ruled. He realized that living was not just a matter of staying alive—it was one of fighting for one's beliefs.

One day Roman met an old friend, a senior officer from his ship, who was a very good electrician. He told Roman that he was making a heating apparatus for "those things that curl the hair. Like scissors… curlers." It was the custom in Russia for men to put curlers around their moustaches to curl them up, like a villain's.

This friend painted a grand picture, "A mustache is the last word in creating a handsome man," he claimed as he swiped the generous growth above his upper lip. "It is a symbol of elegance. A straggly, drooping, unkempt mustache is the property only of the slovenly, the unmannered and the ignorant. Such a poor mustache declares its owner to be a person without any sense of fashion or self-respect. But, a well-cut and well-groomed mustache bespeaks of a proud man, who knows his self-worth. You can make a fortune selling these curlers. You just have to heat up the curler on something hot being careful you don't overheat it and burn yourself. Then you just curl the mustache. But… be careful."

The friend asked Roman to travel around Crimea selling the curling iron. Roman tried that for a while but he didn't like it. Not only couldn't he stand being stranded ashore any longer, he didn't like the selling. It was difficult to heat the iron to the right temperature and you could easily burn yourself. When he learned that the White forces pathetically fighting the Bolsheviks had gathered a few ships together but needed men to run them, Roman knew instantly what he must do: he had to join up once more to fight the only way he knew, at sea, aboard some ship. *I'm a seaman not a salesman.*

Roman walked to the corner and turned down the next street towards the harbor. With increasing frequency for the last several weeks he'd walked to the harbor to stare out at the ships that had once made up Russia's Black Sea fleet. It was so depleted now. Less than half the number of ships berthed here a year ago were still here.

It's so different from how everything used to be! I can only see parts of the ships, their masts still poking above water... their hulls resting on the harbor bottom. I wonder whose orders scuttled them?

Roman felt physical pain every time he came here, but he couldn't stay away. He was drawn to the water. Once again he came to sit on a little bench at the pier's edge, to stare and remember how he'd arrived at this unsettled point in his life. With a sad heart, he turned his eyes to the *Empress Maria's* great hump rising out of the water. Destroyed.

Roman slowly rose from the bench, without enthusiasm, and walked away.

The "Captain" he'd talked to last night had asked Roman to meet him today at the end of another pier like this one. He'd told Roman, "There's a new navy being born." But Roman knew it would never be like the one when he'd served aboard the *Empress Maria*. Those days were gone forever. The Russia he knew was gone. Making his decision, Roman went to his old friend, his boss. "I hate selling," he declared bluntly. "The curlers are fine, but I'm not a salesman. I'm a seaman. I need a ship. I have decided to join the White navy."

"We do not have a navy!"

"Yes, we do! We are forming one."

"You are? With what?"

"With whatever we can find. What's left of the big fleet, little boats—whatever floats."

Chapter 22

In the fall of 1918 with no rigid governmental structure anywhere in Russia, chaos continued to increase. The Red Guard arrested Xenia's father during this time. Harvey was still desperately trying to keep the newspaper going—not end it. From time to time when he got free information, he continued to print it. While Harvey was in prison, Xenia stayed with her mother in Moscow and was allowed to take food to her father in prison.

The anarchists were among the earliest and most outspoken critics of the Bolsheviks. They were against the ruling power and authority in general. From time to time they printed notices, little newspapers and leaflets on Harvey's presses. They said, "Please help us, we have to fight the Reds." He himself was not an anarchist at the beginning of the revolution—but many of his neighbors were—so he allowed them to use his presses. Harvey was willing to do what he could, as long as he could, against the Bolsheviks. Then he was arrested and taken to prison.

In early October, when the anarchists learned Harvey had been arrested, they stormed the prison where he was housed. Armed with machine guns, they liberated him. Anarchists were still quite strong at this time, so it was possible for them to use such force. The Communists, the Reds, were afraid of them at that time.

Once liberated, Harvey went into hiding outside of Moscow.

Because Xenia had worked with her father at the newspaper, there was the possibility the Reds might come after her. The family decided she would be safer if she went with her Uncle Edward. He was a naval officer and an engineer, who had come through Moscow from the Baltic Sea, and was staying at their house. He and a number of the naval officers were going south to join with the Whites in the area where Roman was—although Xenia didn't know it. She'd had no word of Roman since July.

Edward stayed in Moscow for a while and, as he prepared to depart, they asked him to take Xenia with him to the grandmother's estate in the southern part of Russia near Voronezh. They'd heard that region area was not yet in as much turmoil as they were experiencing in Moscow.

Once Xenia and her uncle were aboard the train, her mother and the rest of the family went to the Volga region to stay with family. It was still a very rich food-producing area while famine and strikes were increasing throughout most of Russia.

Xenia and her young uncle Edward,--about 27 years old—traveled in baggage cars, sitting on the floor. It was about 100 miles to their destination so they brought a basket with some bread and sandwiches.

Xenia said to her uncle, "We look terrible." He easily agreed. "At the next big station, I'll go to the barber. There will also be a restaurant and everything there. I have some money, so you can buy something nice."

At the station, Xenia felt extremely apprehensive as she waited for her uncle to return. As the train was about to leave and Edward wasn't back, she frantically ran to find him. "The train is leaving!" she yelled at him.

"I'm ready," he replied calmly as he watched the train leave without them.

Xenia was devastated—and angry. "All our luggage is on the train. I don't have my British passport with all the eagles and my picture on it…and everything else. It's there in my suitcases… and our basket of food…everything is there on the train," she lamented. "What can we do?"

"Never mind, I have a lot of money so we can buy something from the peasants coming here to the station to sell their goods. We'll just get another train," he said easily. "How nice to just relax and do nothing," he said with a sigh while stretching his arms. Xenia was biting her lip, worried.

It was a long wait—about seven hours—before another train came. By then Xenia was exhausted and discouraged. Finally, they reached their destination about 50 miles from Voronezh, the large regional city. From there they worked their way to the estate of her grandmother on her mother's side and told her their troubles.

"Grandmother, we have nothing," cried Xenia as her grandmother tried to calm her. It was then Xenia learned that although they had nothing, there was something worse: Edward had a gun which he'd hidden in a small thin oil can and sealed it shut. He was now anxious about their things still on the train.

The grandmother was very old and didn't fully comprehend the situation with the revolution. Her husband, Xenia's grandfather, had been one of the gardeners to the Emperor. He had passed away by then and the grandmother was a pleasant, but naïve 80 years-old lady still living in relative comfort. She assured Xenia, "The Emperor will send someone from St. Petersburg. Everything will be all right!" Because she still had money, she'd built the peasants a church and schools. She was well liked and cared for but was not aware of the political situation.

Xenia's aunt was also at the estate and was more practical than the grandmother. She knew more of what was happening. She suggested that Xenia and Uncle Edward go to Voronezh. "Tell officials that some people knew you were coming to Voronezh and must have taken their luggage off for you. I'll go with you to help you find your things at the station," the aunt volunteered.

Earlier on the train, Xenia and her uncle had spoken to a nice lady. In their conversations, they'd told her where they were going and divided their food with her.

At the station Xenia discretely asked some questions and reported back, "Auntie, it turns out that because of this nice lady, only our basket was taken and the rest of our things have been put into a safety deposit box in the station." Upon learning this, the aunt was very angry. "You are too light-hearted. Go get your things." She was worried because their names were on their things. The uncle was reluctant to do that; he just wanted to walk around for a while enjoying his freedom. Finally, he agreed, "Okay...come on, Xenia, let's go."

There were already Red Guards at the station. Xenia and her uncle were stopped without any questions being asked and ordered to go to the local Communist police station. The police first questioned the uncle because they had their suspicions about him. There were quite a few people at the police station asking too many questions to suit the uncle so he told them he was an engineer going from Leningrad to this location to visit his family and friends.

He said that he had been wounded during the war. He also claimed that he was very musically inclined and he had a violin that he was worried about. Actually, the uncle had hidden the can with the gun and all his money inside the violin. Although the violin looked intact, he was concerned that

---

Voronezh

One of most picturesque and provincial cities of Russia, Voronezh lies in what is known as the Black Earth region, southeast of St. Petersburg (Petrograd) and approximately 250 miles south of Moscow. It lies above the steep banks of the Voronezh River.

Of major importance, the Voronezh River flows through the city onward to a point about 25 miles downstream, meeting the Don River which flows through much of European Russia.

Voronezh was founded principally as a multi-towered fortress by Czar Feodar in 1585 and 1586 as a protection against nomadic tribes. Some claim that previous settlements in the same area can be traced as far back as the Stone Age.

It was here, too, that Peter the Great later established a shipbuilding yard and the first Russian Naval fleet. A major factor in the city's early development was this position of being an apex of important transport routes. In 1871, rails connected Voronezh to Moscow.

Voronezh has always been known for its cultural achievements, industry, and, of course, agriculture. Through the years many famous people have come from this region including poets and writers such as Tolstoi and Chekhov.

The city was destroyed three times by fire, but always rebuilt. It never gave up.

they would find the money and the gun, then arrest him and possibly shoot him.

Finally, he became really worried about his and Xenia's situation and took it seriously.

While all of 1918 had been a time of change, suspicions were heightened, and danger increased daily during October.

Xenia tried to appear calm as she and her aunt were told to get out. The fellow in charge wanted to talk to the uncle alone and ask him some special questions. Xenia rationalized to her aunt, "Right now, I don't think these Bolsheviks are blood-thirsty...well... maybe not *so* blood-thirsty. I think the higher-ups are more blood-thirsty, but those under them mostly want money and all kinds of advantages." Her aunt gave her a look and was strangely quiet.

The man questioning her uncle actually did just want money. The uncle was clever enough to bargain with some of his money and ended up giving him some of the "new money" in exchange saying he would take his luggage later.

Meanwhile, Xenia went to the police department for her luggage while the aunt waited. There was a young man sitting at the table. It turned out he was the brother of the man investigating her uncle. Xenia envisioned him as a very nice fellow. "May I have my luggage?" Xenia asked politely. But inwardly she panicked when he said, "That depends, you know. I think so. But first, I must examine your luggage." She was terrified because of her British passport. Since she and her uncle had left the train, they might be thought of as spies. Many British and French during this time were being accused of being spies. *I must collect my wits and show my concern.*

The fellow said, "I'll help you. "

Xenia smiled and started to take everything out of her suitcase—shoes, underwear, and the ladies' things—all the while doing flirtatious actions to distract him and hoping to embarrass him. She mussed things up enough that she managed to get her passport and papers into her pocket without him seeing her actions.

Laughingly, she said to the fellow, "...well, well...you can see nothing is here. It's nonsense, you know!"

At last they were free to go and the ordeal was finished—or so Xenia thought.

Chapter 23

Xenia felt fairly safe at the estate because of its distance of about thirteen miles out of Voronezh and not an area of fighting. She stayed there with her grandmother several different times during the next two years into the spring of 1919. The estate offered more security and sufficient food than Moscow. She often worried about Roman, but had no idea where either he or her friend, Kira, was during this time.

Then conditions changed. Rapidly. As the White Forces advanced toward Moscow to fight with the Reds, the estate was no longer secure. The Reds—the Soviets—desperately needed more forces and unexpectedly invaded the estate.

Girls from the adjoining estates were forced to the front lines to dig ditches. But, Xenia's skills exempted her from the digging. She was forced back to Moscow to work in an office for the Soviets. And she hated every minute. Middle class people and students were also forced by the Reds to work for them in the cities. It was a time of desperation.

During the summer, having heard rumors that White troops were closer to Moscow, Xenia and thirteen or fourteen others from her office decided to take a chance and cross the lines hoping to escape to the White army. Xenia expressed to them, "We know that the Reds really are not very nice people, so with the White forces coming, let's run away from the Reds and try to get to the south into the Caucasus Mountains. My godmother is living there." Then Xenia hoped to join her mother and her siblings now in Dubovka, situated on the Volga River.

"Let's go." The group readily agreed to leave immediately. Hurriedly, they began walking along the nearest road. Naively, they didn't try to scatter and hide as they went. When they saw a cavalry detachment, they excitedly ran toward them thinking they were Whites—only to find they were Cossacks—the Reds. Xenia and the rest of the group were instantly surrounded and harshly ordered to dig a large grave. "Bigger. Keep digging until we tell you," the Reds ordered. They stood back and watched with no expressions of compassion in their demeanor. They stood around in their dirty uniforms smoking and laughing while the group dug.

Some of the group whimpered and begged; others were white with fear as they dug their own grave. They knew they were going to die, but they had to continue. Even though it was summer, the soil was still hard and they had to struggle with each shovel full of dirt they took out of the ground.

"That's enough. Stop." The Reds were finally satisfied. The captors then placed a large board across the grave and ordered the entire group to stand on it. "Now. Hurry up," They demanded without any sign of feeling. Amid the anguished cries of terror and streaming tears, prayers were on everyone's lips. There was no reprieve. One by one they walked across the board with legs that hardly held them up.

The firing began. In turn, each was shot and fell into the mass grave. Xenia cried, "Oh, God, how can this be? I don't even get to tell Roman how much I love him. I don't even know if he's alive...Oh, my family..."

Xenia fell into the grave with the other bodies.

Silence—except for the laughter of the Reds.

Chapter 24

Roman knew nothing about the slaughter of Xenia's group. His focus was on the "new" navy and he still hadn't tried to contact her or his family. He realized at the outset that service in this new navy—pieced together by the White forces with parts from other ships—would be nothing like his earlier service in the Black Sea Fleet. For one thing, the Imperial Russian Navy was no more, neither in name nor actuality. Its ships lay partly or totally submerged in Sevastopol and other harbors, scuttled to keep the Germans from acquiring them.

Nowhere was this more painfully felt by Roman than when he looked nostalgically, as he did almost every day, at the most symbolic scene of all: the barnacled, upturned hulk of the *Empress Maria*, his first home at sea. Once she had been the centerpiece of Russia's Navy; now she peeped above the water line like an overturned bathtub. *Oh how my life has changed.*

Roman had become a fugitive threatened with execution; had lolled around in a winery as a lookout; and had been an accomplice in a kidnapping. Now, he was abandoned like an unwanted child in sight of his first-ever naval assignment. It was a sad view of his naval career.

True, he was aboard a ship again this fall of 1918—on a gunboat armed with twenty six-inch guns—and at sea with the White Navy. But, it was nothing like he had once envisioned his career would be. It certainly wasn't as glorious as his career had begun aboard the *Empress Maria*.

Roman thought of how everything in his world was different. Nothing was the same this year as before. Russia—the old Russia in which he had grown up—was as demolished as the *Empress Maria*. The nation had suffered irreparable damage during the last four years of the

Great War: she had signed away preposterous quantities of land and people to Germany with the Brest-Litovsk Treaty; and had convulsed daily during the Bolshevik takeover. The brutal aftermath continued. This endless Civil War had made Roman's homeland as damaged a hulk of its former self as the *Empress Maria*.

Roman's thoughts grew worse as he remembered again the events of only a few weeks ago. *How quickly it had all happened.* The last hope of a return to a monarchy with a Czar at its head had died in July in the basement of the house in Ekaterinburg where thugs had murdered Nicholas II and his family one by one. That monstrous act was the last insult the Bolsheviks could throw at Russia. The murders ended Imperial Russia with all its glory—art, drama, leisurely walks through beautiful parks, and fine dinners with friends. Yet, by the grace of God, Roman was still alive and back at sea, but disheartened. *What is to come? I don't see much hope...How is my family...and Xenia?*

At the moment, he stood despondently at the railing of the gunboat as it plowed westward along the Black Sea coastline just west of the Crimea. It was heading toward Odessa and Nikolayev, patrolling for any sign of Red troops that might have infiltrated this far south from Petrograd and Moscow. As best he could, Roman sought food for the crews of his own and other gunboats. All that greeted him, though, was the repetition of emaciated faces of people in the villages he passed, standing in rags as he came ashore. He was finding greater trouble at each village, because the people who stared mutely at him as he begged were worse off than he. Finally he could stand no more of such suffering. He ceased going ashore, and just sailed slowly by.

"How can I beg food from people who are begging for food themselves?" he told his first mate, Gregori Mattloff. "It's senseless! And there is no fighting for us at sea, because the Reds have even fewer ships than we do."

True, the Reds had no navy. Fighting these days was between armies. Roman had heard just last night that the Reds were gradually pushing the White armies eastward, although he could see no sign of infantry or cavalry forces. Yet, it was common knowledge that Bolshevik forces lately were increasing in strength. They were overcoming the White armies under *Lieutenant General* Anton Denikin with greater ease at every encounter. Roman sensed it would be only a matter of time.

Then, another change brought new hope. Orders came for Roman to move his boat eastward. There was urgent need for him and other patrols to bolster support for advancing White troops who were actually beating back Reds along the Don and Volga rivers. Unfortunately, the hope was short-lived. Red troops that had been tied up fighting Germans were now freed under the 1918 Armistice as the

Germans retreated westward; Bolshevik forces were thus strengthened even more and the tide of battle turned back in their favor once more.

As odd and pitiful as the White Navy was, Roman was beginning to recognize the blessing of being back at sea. After all, he had endured for the last two years, he was still alive. More often these days he thanked God for his life.

In the shifting tides of the fighting on land, the makeshift White flotilla supported the White armies as best they could. However, they were relentlessly forced to move east as the Bolshevik forces beat their way to the edge of the Crimea. The Whites were pushed toward the Sea of Azov and beyond, into the Caucasus. With the fighting focused along the River Don and the Volga,

"Why aren't you in the army?"

Volunteer Army recruitment poster during the Russian Civil War. The Volunteer Army existed from 1918 till 1920. Anton Denikin was the commander of the 1st Division of this army.   (Wikipedia)

Roman and the few other remaining ships were ordered into that particular theater of war in an attempt to stem the Red tide.

Battles raged back and forth for months in the Don and Volga

regions. Bit by bit, Reds with their increased forces beat the Whites on land ever eastward, toward Siberia. The White troops under Anton Denikin were too few and too poorly armed to prolong any victory.

Roman kept up with what was happening with the White Volunteer Army through his fellow officers who were in charge of other gunboats. What happened to the army determined the fate of the navy.

With increasing frequency during the past few months, Roman had heard that Denikin fought even harsher internal battles against many of his own officers than against the Reds— particularly General Baron Pyotr Wrangel. A cavalry commander with great charisma and equally great military skills, Wrangel was perpetually at odds with Denikin. The two men had totally different strategies. It eventually came to the point where Denikin simply ordered Wrangel out of the country and later called him a traitor.

Troops on both sides were forced into idleness as heavy snows blanketed the land during the extremely harsh winter of 1918-1919. Still, the Reds managed to bring increasing pressure against the Whites, eventually owning the Crimea and all the area east of that strategic peninsula. They continued to crowd the Whites down the Volga into Caspian Sea waters. In March, 1919, the White Navy arrived fully into the Caspian theater of war when a detachment of officers and men from the Black Sea Fleet arrived at Petrovsky on the Caspian's northern shore. With this, the character of the war changed drastically for Roman. He experienced some hope.

The White Navy was again at war on an open sea rather than the limiting confines of river warfare. However, the greatest difference was the presence of British, French, Italian, and Turkish forces, all of whom were grasping for the same gold: the millions of barrels of oil beneath the sea. The Allies combined their forces to prevent the oil from reaching Germany. Turkey, alone, tried futilely to supply Germany. This confrontation continued although the Great War was history by 1919 when the White Navy first put in its appearance in the Caspian.

Chapter 25

Xenia tried to open her eyes. Her head felt as if flies were buzzing around inside. Then she felt the weight of a body across her legs. As she began to recall the horror, she wanted desperately to close it out. She heard no sounds. Nothing. She finally sensed she hadn't been shot: at least she didn't have any pain. Xenia continued the silence as she became more alert and then listened for any noise in the grave. Still nothing. *I must have fainted a split second before a bullet hit me. I'm in the grave with all my murdered friends. Oh, God...am I really the only one alive?* Then she heard the sound of a quiet movement in the grave.

A young man whispered, "Are you okay? I'm wounded, but not badly. It seems all the others are dead."

She returned the whisper, "I think I'm okay, but I don't think anyone else is alive. Oh, God. How can this be?" Xenia quietly sobbed.

Fearfully the two listened. The captors seemed to have moved on. Silently they waited for the cover of darkness. Seeing no movement in the bodies of their friends and hearing no voices, the young man helped Xenia over the tangled, bleeding bodies and into the woods. He whispered to her again, "We must stay hidden through the night and hope they don't return."

In the morning they moved cautiously onward until they found refuge among some helpful peasants who shared a little of the food they had with them. Then they parted, cautiously going in different directions not caring about their dirty and bloody appearances.

Traveling alone now, Xenia continued her attempt to escape the Soviets. After tidying up as best she could she tried to get back to Moscow by train but ended up in Voronezh. She knew of other relatives in the area, but not how to reach them. Just as she arrived in Voronezh, the Cossacks and troops marched into town. Terrified, she didn't know what to do when they detained her, but some people helped her. She is allowed to go free because of her British papers. Exhausted, she managed to return to her grandmother's estate. There she cried and cried, finding comfort in hugging her grandmother. She told her everything, including her latest close call. "There was chaos everywhere. The Red army was passing by and dragging artillery. They were running away from the White forces because the Reds weren't prepared for them. I didn't have anything. No money, nothing. I only had my British passport. I never thought I would get here."

By October the White armies had taken over Voronezh. Food became more scarce everywhere. Adding to starvation, typhus and cholera were epidemic. Xenia was not spared; she became seriously ill with typhus.

By November, when the Whites were defeated in Moscow, a weakened Xenia set out to find her parents in the Volga region, despite the chaotic train conditions. The only papers she carried, hidden, were her British passport and an old paper saying she was working as a clerk in the Reds' office. In actuality, the passport had expired. Xenia was still naïve, but hoped to fool any Reds she came in contact with.

At first Xenia traveled in a big luggage car, more like a cattle car. She just sat there, ill and very miserable, trying to endure the penetrating cold and not breathe in the heavy dust. The girl who brought her to the station—one of her friends from near the estate who had been forced to dig until the Reds moved on—had brought her some boiled potatoes. But Xenia was so hungry that she ate all the potatoes at once: she had nothing left. Even her blanket was too small to keep her warm. She felt barely alive.

Xenia observed the many people on the floor along with the luggage, and in between them was a small coal burner and a kettle for water. Those that were able just sat around it trying to warm themselves. But, Xenia found very little room for herself. On the sides of the car were a couple of benches. On one of them, Xenia saw a very beautiful lady reclining on nice, clean pillows. Beside her, a fellow in military attire attended to her, talking. The lady noticed Xenia and realized she wasn't one of the peasants. "You poor little girl. Where are you going?"

"I'm going to the Volga region to join my family." When she asked if Xenia wanted something, Xenia responded, "No thank you." and nothing more. After that the lady often talked to her. Sometimes she gave her tea or some bread. Xenia appreciated the kindness and thought her appearance probably raised the sympathy.

This same lady told the military man near her, "In about two hours both you and the young lady will be changing trains and going to the same city. Will you please take care of her?" Xenia hadn't paid much attention to him before: She was too exhausted from her illness.

The military man first helped Xenia off when the train reached the station and then continued on his way. As Xenia sat waiting for another train, two bedraggled soldiers come up to her. She noticed with some relief that they didn't have any insignias. One came up and said, "Oh, sister". Xenia hesitated before asking, "What?" He didn't look familiar to her. Then he said, "You were my nurse in the hospital. I remember you nursing me in Moscow in 1916. You look so poorly. Are you sick?"

Surprised, she responded, "I have been very ill."

"Where are you going?" he queried. When Xenia told him, he said, "We're not going to the same place, but we're going in the same direction as you. We'll embark on the same train as you are and we'll help you. What kind of papers do you have?"

Xenia reluctantly gave him the information and became nervous when it turned out this former patient was a Bolshevik commander. When he saw her papers, he told his orderly to go into the office and type a letter, "This nurse is traveling with us."

Xenia thought to herself, *maybe this will help me go on my way, to get on this train.* The train was completely full but they got Xenia on and stuck her next to a window. Her benefactors then forced themselves around her, standing. She thought, *They can't even sit. It's awful.*

In a short time, Xenia's benefactors reached their destination and she thanked them, relieved she could be on her way. Now, she needed to change to another train, so she discarded her large bag and changed her things into only one bag. The large bag was too heavy for her to carry in her weakened condition: she could barely manage the small one.

At this station, Xenia stood on the platform—not quite sure where to go—when she heard someone say, "Oh, isn't that the little girl?" Turning around, Xenia saw the same military officer who had helped her at an earlier time. He was now assisting a well-known actress board her train to Moscow. He then invited Xenia to come with him as he headed toward a special track. Xenia thought, *it's strange that there is only a single rail car there.*

Another soldier carried the officer's luggage to the single car and indicated that she should follow him inside. Nervously she followed. Once inside, she now realized that one part of the car is an infirmary and the remaining part dedicated to military "high brass" and other Red Guard. Conversations indicated they are traveling to the same town on the Volga River, Saratov, as Xenia because that area is where many Germans have lived and raised much of the needed wheat and other crops.

Xenia realized at that moment that the military were being sent there to take everything they could and clean out the region – all the wheat and supplies. *I don't know what to do.*

There were quite a few people: some of them old; some of them military; some women. One lady kept talking—seemingly to everyone—and how she hated all those "*White* people, *White* Forces, officers, and everybody. "They are so terrible. They killed my brother." She continued denouncing them. Xenia thought the lady was a very bad woman and disliked her, but she kept her mouth closed. She was afraid to say anything.

The single car was now hooked to a train and started out slowly. Xenia was frightened that night when two soldiers and the conductor come to the car and asked for tickets or passes. Everybody handed them over. When they come to Xenia, she was shaking but trying to appear calm. She is then told she doesn't have sufficient papers. They told her, "Well, citizen, it is not enough. Come, *tovarich*, Comrade, it is not enough. Don't you have anything more? " When she quietly tells them "no" she is told she'll have to go with them. Xenia attempts to control her panic and doesn't argue.

Xenia left her luggage and followed them to another car—the car for prisoners. She is informed that in the morning at the next station there is a special police department and they will investigate her. "It's strange that you're traveling on this train, in that compartment without any documents or papers."

The officer who'd brought her wasn't there at that time and didn't know she was being taken. Xenia waited. In the morning, the soldiers came for her and took her to the police station—the same kind as the one in Voronezh when she and her uncle had been detained.

Xenia tried to talk naturally and told them she was going to see her family and how "those terrible White forces are forcing me out and I had to...." She let out a little nervous chuckle. The interrogators hesitated, then told her she looked "suspicious". At that moment her rescuer, the nice Commander, came in and told them she was under his protection. He claimed he was taking her to be his secretary where he was going. The Commander was asked who he was and said, "Show us your papers."

Satisfied, they told the benefactor, "She might be trouble." He replied, "Never mind, she's under my protection." Xenia realized he must have been very important, because the interrogators answered, "All right. It's up to you." He took her back to the car.

Everybody stared at Xenia when she returned to the car. Suddenly, the young girl looked at her and started to weep, really crying. Xenia had a change of heart and felt sorry for her. She even offered to get her some water and medicine. "Perhaps we should go to the infirmary and get you some medicine. You don't look well."

At the entrance to the infirmary, the girl started to embrace Xenia and whispered, "I thought you were a spy, and I am running away. My father is a general and I was just trying to tell them all kinds of terrible stories to make them think I'm on their side. I saw you looking at me so suspiciously that I thought you were a spy. And when they arrested you, I knew who you were *not* one of them."

Xenia told her own story and they sat together in the empty infirmary talking quietly. Although Xenia was extremely tired after her ordeal, they returned to the car acting as if there was nothing different.

Xenia became uncomfortable when she noticed an older officer kept staring at her. Finally, he said, "Well, *tovarich,* it's very nice that young commander is so eager to help you." Again, the helpful commander was somewhere else, maybe smoking. Then this older officer said, "But, we have to investigate anyway, because—you know—on the way we just arrested three spies and you look suspicious to me. I want to look into your luggage."

What can I do, Xenia pondered. Then she said, "Yes, but let me wash my hands and face first because I feel so dusty." She quickly picked up her "necessary" little bag and said, as she headed to the wash room before he could stop her, "In a minute, I'll be with you."

In the restroom, she tore her passport into pieces and, seeing a small stove, she burned the pieces. Then she went back and calmly said, "How about now?" He looked straight at her saying, "I don't think it's necessary now. No, I don't think it's necessary." He knew what she'd done, but she'd done it so quickly he couldn't do anything. He just looked at her. Xenia thought, *He's a very experienced old fox.*

The train finally arrived at their destination and in the half-hour before they could disembark, the older officer said he wanted to speak to Xenia. She knew she'd better comply.

Outside the train, on the little platform, the officer waited for Xenia and said, "How about going to work for me? I need someone like you. You are very clever. You outwitted even *me,* an experienced officer... and I am the Chief of Secret Police."

When Xenia didn't say anything, he continued, "I am being sent from Leningrad to the capitol of the Volga Region" He paused, then asked, "How about coming to work for me as my secretary? You will be all right."

Xenia slowly responded while trying to maintain a pleasant look on her face, "Yes, but I need to recover from an illness and have to rest. I can't start work right away. But I'll be here staying with an aunt." She feared he would find out about her family, so she gave him a fake address. "I'll come to you in about two days," she said with a smile.

"All right. Here's the address where to report," he said.

Xenia thanked him and left with her one suitcase. She waved as she headed in the direction of the fake address. As soon as she knew she wasn't followed, she hastened her steps to her aunt's and the welcoming arms of family. Bursting into the house, Xenia gasped, "You must hide me and not let the Reds Know I am here." With that she collapsed.

Chapter 26

On a sunny but frigid winter day in March, 1919, Roman had his first view of the Caspian Sea. He was standing on a pier in Petrovosky, a port on the sea's northwest shore south of Astrakhan and the Volga delta. He and his gunboat crew had come by train from the eastern part of the Crimea after they had been released from their days of idling near Kerch where Red and White forces were stalemated.

Roman stared in amazement at the vast sea before him, then murmured in satisfaction, "This is more like real naval sea duty." He'd heard about the famous Caspian Sea all his life, the largest inland sea in the world, stretching almost

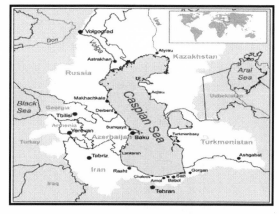

Map from Wikipedia

800 miles from north to south and touching Russian, Turkish and Persian lands. It was nothing like where they'd been. Life on the Don and Volga rivers where they had supported White armies, seesawing back and forth against the Reds, had been limited at best.

There was no room for the larger warships; gunboat duty was mostly patrolling.

The only guns they had were much smaller than Roman had been accustomed to aboard the *Empress Maria* or the *Empress Catherine the Great*. Hopefully, here on the Caspian he would find some larger ships.

163

The Bolsheviks had pushed the White armies down the rivers and other revolutionary forces had swept through the Ukraine and the northern part of the Crimea but came up short near Kerch. They'd been waiting for days for reinforcements from areas where serious military opposition had been wiped out.

Here in the Caspian, British forces were mostly in control—but were undermanned—so they welcomed the arrival of these White officers and crews. Control of the Caspian was vital in order to capture as much oil as possible from the vast undersea reserves—not for conquest of land. Turkish units repeatedly attempted to transport oil from the eastern shores to the Germans, but, the British officers explained, this was minor now since the Armistice. The main goal for the Russians, according to the British officers briefing the new arrivals, was to prevent Red forces from shutting down Britain's shipments of oil via pipeline from Baku to its ports on the Black Sea for its own uses.

Roman was wary and didn't have a good feeling. *Something is wrong.* He expressed to one of his fellow crewmen, "I have the distinct feeling that the British, wise and strong as they are militarily, are really rather naive in their understanding of the Bolsheviks. Most of the world beyond Russia's borders seems to be the same way. I think the revolution against the czar and the former Russian empire is clearly an attempt to impose Bolshevism on the world."

He continued, "After these months of brutal civil warfare, it's clear to me that the Bolsheviks are fast becoming Russia's new, permanent government even though their rise to power is riddled with horrors."

As welcome as they were meant to feel by the British, the officers and crewmen with Roman were not too happy with the state of things. The British were undermanned; the Reds were inexorably pushing White forces down the Volga; and they were nearing the river delta.

A large force of Cossacks under a Col. Bicharakov had taken independent steps to create a navy of their own. They needed to deal with the Turks who repeatedly tried to carry oil cargoes to their own bases and eventually to Germany. The British officers declared the

Cossack crews were unreliable. This situation became most noticeable within weeks of Roman's arrival, when Admiral Norris, commander of the British Caspian naval forces, disarmed the Cossacks and assumed responsibility for operations against the Reds. The Russians had to scrape together a lot of castoff ships and put them in fighting condition. Roman was assigned to a cruiser and, for a short while they—the Whites—managed to hold the Red forces back.

Roman was aware that the Reds had also established a navy using some ships, including old destroyers transferred from the Baltic, and thus dealt heavy blows to the Whites.

Eventually the Reds pushed into the Caspian proper. The next several months turned out to be the most fearful of all of Roman's experiences. The British retreated, all the way down the Caspian to Baku. In the summer of 1919, the British pulled out, leaving the remnants of the White forces to fend for themselves.

Several hundred White sailors and a few officers' families and other anti-Bolshevik supporters crowded into what ships they could get hold of and fled south to Anzali near the Persian border. They were halted in mid-stride, astoundingly, by their British allies and declared to be Russian civil war combatants. In this strange turn of events, they were searched and all their weapons confiscated. The British thoroughly and completely disarmed them, taking all rifles; even taking the bolts out of them. Then they insisted that they hand over their open knives. They were prohibited from going anywhere, and instead were incarcerated aboard a ship. Then, in another, even more surprising gesture, the British invited Roman and the other Russian officers to have dinner with them. Roman thought this strange but kept this thought to himself.

The British officers are gracious hosts, and pleasant company. But the truth is, we are really British captives, despite the fact that we have been side by side for more than a year. Why is this happening?

The British assured Roman's superior officer that the Reds wouldn't come this far—and if they did—they would not dare to intrude on British domain. Roman didn't agree with their reasoning, but he could do nothing except what he was doing, keeping a watchful eye on the Caspian area they had left behind only a few days ago. *One thing was certain: The Reds are out there and moving closer.*

***

At 6 a.m. May 6, 1920, everyone in the town of Anzali had their answer. The day broke in two distinct ways. Bright sunshine promised a beautiful day, but the thunderous sound of gunfire brought increased terror and confusion. Heavy shelling crashed into the ships in the harbor and the compound on shore. The Reds had found them. They had come down from the Volga River on the Caspian Sea cutting off the main road that conducted traffic from Anzali south. The road went through a very narrow piece of land between the sea and a lake south of Anzali.

Several Bolshevik ships could be seen on the northern horizon. The barrage lasted what seemed an eternity but was really only a few minutes. No one was killed or injured. In the silence that followed those explosions, a guttural shout sounded across the harbor. In English, and directed at the British was heard, "You have enemies of Russia aboard your ship. Release them to us at once. They are criminals who must be brought to justice."

Immediately, Roman was ordered to get his people to the starboard, the shoreward side of the ship away from the Reds who were already sending a landing party armed with machine guns towards the large British ship. British crews were also ready at their own cannons as Roman quickly helped herd people aboard small crafts out of sight of the Reds as much as possible and down gang planks to shore. There were cries of fear from the children and the families of white crews and confusion in the hurry-up scramble. "Quickly. Keep the noise down as much as possible," Roman urged as he took charge.

Then, miraculously, the White group was ashore and hurrying out of sight into the woods beyond the tiny town of Anzali. By the time the Reds' landing party traversed the harbor the British had brought things to a calm appearance. Tension was high but submersed beneath the remarkably calm exteriors of the British officers. When the

166

Bolshevik landing party arrived, they faced the guns of the British and were told, "Stay in your cutter. The White group you are seeking are not here. They have already departed."

Expectedly, the Reds were furious and prepared to depart to chase the fleeing Whites, but the British showed them that they were surrounded by British crewmen, heavily armed. They were also advised that they were trespassing on British held territory, in Persia, beyond Russia's boundaries. In essence, the British detained them on basically the same grounds they had used to hold up Roman's group: This was a no-combat zone: no fighting was allowed within the British jurisdiction.

The Reds boasted they had cut off the main road out of Anzali. But they didn't know of the narrow road along a narrow strip of land between the sea and a lake south of Anzali. A British officer had pointed the way to this road for Roman and his group of several hundred people who hurried breathlessly along it. They were bound toward another little Persian town, Resht. They traveled as quietly as they could, but there were perhaps as many as 400 in the party, and Roman and other officers were concerned they would quickly be found out.

The group traveled for about an hour without being discovered and so continued on for perhaps two more hours before stopping to rest. They were exhausted and beginning to stumble and fall as they fled. "I know you're exhausted, but several crewmen went to scout out the road ahead while you rested and have come with a frightening report: a contingent of soldiers is a mile or so ahead. Terrible news! Now we're trapped with soldiers behind, and soldiers ahead."

Roman made a decision and ordered, "We'll make camp and wait. What else can we do except pray? It's the only thing left."

Suddenly Roman excitedly passed on the word, "I see a boat. An empty boat! With paddle wheels! It's moving slowly in the same direction we were going, toward Resht!"

As the boat approached, Roman hailed it as the group waited tensely and the captain brought it close to shore. After some brief parlaying, the captain told them all to come aboard. His ship wasn't very large, but if people crowded together, they could make it. One of the officers pointed out the four-foot high railing along the ship. If people lay down on top of one another they might not be spotted from land. This they did, lying four and five deep atop one another like pancakes below the railing with little room to breathe. The little paddle-wheeler slowly passed the Red soldiers encamped farther along the lake road. There were long moments as they passed when everyone held their breath fearing the soldiers would want to inspect the boat, but they did nothing more than shout greetings to the captain.

Roman and the entire group made it safely to Resht without discovery. Once there, everyone began selling whatever they were carrying—blankets, excess clothing, whatever they had grabbed when leaving the British ship. The Persians bought all the items quickly, and soon the party was on its way again. They didn't know exactly where they were going, but always south, always to get as far from the Bolsheviks as possible even though they were bone weary and frightened.

This shred of peace was destroyed a short distance out of Resht. Ahead of them, they encountered several army vehicles filled with soldiers waiting for them. They quickly realized they were British, tall dark-skinned men wearing white turbans: Britain's famed Gurkha troops from the Nepal region. This relief, that they were British and therefore friendly, quickly changed into a new anxiety. The soldiers surrounded them, signaling with their guns to halt and gather closer together. After a few moments of stern conversation and protests, the Gurkhas motioned them forward and directed them into a small valley. It was all done with very little talk, merely some blunt commands as the soldiers herded the group together. The most shocking thing was that the British quickly strung barbed wire around the group.

"What are you doing?" shouted Roman. "Why are you treating us like this? We have done nothing. We told you that we just want to escape the Bolshevik rabble!"

The British commanding officer, a tall Gurhka, who spoke with a slight accent but politely, held up one hand. "This is only temporary. We must do this for your safety. There are Persian soldiers about.

They would do worse than this if they found you. Please…Be patient."

Sometime later, after the group had ceased rumbling, the officer told the Russian group, "We have known you were coming. We have heard of Russia's defeat finally by the Bolsheviks. It is too bad. We really have great sympathy for you. But you are exiles now, and you are in a foreign land. We must find out what to do with you. However, we will care for you as best we can. Be assured of that." He waited a few moments, ramrod straight, with no expression on his heavily mustached face. Eventually, his face smoothed into an official smile, and without another word he turned around and strode away.

Roman fumed, but there was nothing more to be said.

Shortly, the British brought some rations to the makeshift compound. Eventually after a long wait, several army trucks appeared and the armed soldiers motioned for the refugee group to climb aboard.

Clearly the refugees were now captives of the British.

Chapter 27

Xenia managed to leave Saratov and return safely to Moscow to live with her father. She felt her place was with him and thought she could help him. However, by January 1920 the Whites were in retreat. By May, they had thoroughly lost control.

During the Civil War years, priests were killed and all church buildings, funds, and property were confiscated. But, for several years, the Church had still remained a powerful social force.

However, an early target of the Revolution was the Russian Orthodox Church. Churches were pillaged and destroyed as Red Army soldiers removed icons and religious objects from chapels. Many priests disappeared and some secretly hid as many valuables as possible out of reach of the Reds. The church was no longer a place of sanctuary.

Churches and their functions were considered by the Bolshevik government to be the "opiate of the people". The Bolsheviks were determined to separate them from both the state and education. Even atheist parades were organized in the streets of large cities.

What was left of the valuable objects remaining in the churches themselves were finally confiscated by official decree about February 1922.

Despite this, sometime in early 1921, Xenia became active in an underground church in Moscow. She was determined to do her part. Bravely, she joined a group of Christians who met secretly for prayer and services each morning at 6:30 a.m. It was necessary to meet clandestinely as the Bolsheviks had closed all the Orthodox churches. Each morning, as she set out early from home, she attempted to act natural and unconcerned, making sure she wasn't being followed. Yet, she knew not to look around. She walked briskly as if on an errand and went different routes to their underground cellar.

It was at this secret meeting place that Xenia met Father Mikhail who had come from Sebastopol where he'd conducted services just before the revolution. He was now leading an underground group in Moscow.

Father Mikhail had been kneeling in prayer at his church in Sevastopol one morning when three sailors quietly entered and snuck up behind him. Carrying rocks hidden in their hands, they intended to kill him. As they closed in he turned to face them and said, in a calm voice, "If you want to stone me to death, go ahead." His words astounded and shamed the sailors. They dropped their rocks and fled from the church.

In Russia, no one was safe. Danger existed everywhere; fear hovered like fog as a constant companion; it was a time of terror.

Xenia considered Father Mikhail a remarkable man; a very perceptive and brave priest. His courage gave Xenia great faith in him and she felt comfortable telling him about Roman.

During these years that Roman and Xenia had been apart they worried about each other, not knowing if they would ever see each other again or even what was happening to the other. There had been no communication for several years.

Chapter 28

Basra

Roman, and the several hundred people from the Caspian Sea, spent hours in the British army trucks before reaching their destination. Dusty, dirty and exhausted they arrived in Basra, a city at the head of the Persian Gulf. It was an agonizing, rattling ride that resulted in frequent stops to care for crying children and weary adults, along with several older people weakened by age and ailments. Some didn't make it and were buried along the way. There wasn't even time to mourn.

Basra was to become these Russians' home for the next eight months, but they never even saw the city proper. Already labeled by the British as "the Caspian Flotilla," the refugees only knew that this was a wholly different world from the one they had just fled. The people here were swarthy, dressed in robes and turbans; and those who came by the compound outside the city stared at the refugees suspiciously. The British kept them separate, guarded them carefully, and kept the Gurkha colonel's promise to treat them well. Yet, the Russians' greatest feeling of safety came from knowing that the Bolsheviks weren't anywhere around.

Other than what the Gurkha officer had told them, they still had no idea why they were here. Roman was puzzled and kept querying as many of the British officers as he could approach. No one ever ventured any additional information—but Roman was persistent. Always, the attitude was "You are Russians. You have been fighting, but you lost. You can't fight any more."

The unbearable heat continued day and night. The refugees' only shelters were some tarpaulins stretched over poles to make tent-like awnings. That provided only the merest bit of relief from the sun during the day and even less from the heat at night.

Those survivors of Roman's group were kept separate from other prisoners in the compound, because, Roman was told repeatedly, they were all part of that famous Russian Revolution, and thus were dangerous. The prisoners found that laughable. The remainder of the roughly four hundred sailors, officers, families and children were clearly unable to have revolted against anyone. They were a shabby, raggedy lot of castoffs, too impoverished, too weak, too stunned by their own fate to influence the fate of anyone else. However, they were treated kindly and fed well enough. British soldiers watched them constantly, making it always clear that they were prisoners, no matter how well treated. The very worst part of the confinement was that it continued for so long without the British giving any good reason. Roman felt not a glimmer of hope.

After months, Roman and several other fellow officers finally confronted the British camp commander demanding an explanation. The British officer, a colonel, a Scotsman named Smith, gave them no satisfaction, so they threatened him in no uncertain terms: "If you don't do anything for us, we're going to *bur-r-r-n* your whole camp! Just *bu-r-r-r-n* it!." Roman stretched out his mocking of the officer's brogue; "We don't care about *you-r-r* camp, but you will have to answer to your government as to why we *bu-r-r-r-ned* it!"

The colonel did not doubt the Russians' determination to make good their threat.

"Do you understand my English?" Roman hurled at the colonel. At first he received only a stony stare from Col. Smith, but finally, he nodded curtly and suppressing a smile, he replied, "Very clearly. Arrangements are being made for you to leave tomorrow or the day after."

The colonel kept his word. A couple of days later several military trucks drew up to the compound with orders that everyone was to load up. "Quickly. The trucks would be leaving in half an hour."

With people jammed into the backs of the transports, the drivers took them on a dusty ride that finally ended at Basra's great harbor where the Tigris and Euphrates rivers meet at the Persian Gulf. The refugees gasped at the size of the port. They saw a vast body of water filled with vessels of every size, shape and nationality. The British convoy pulled onto a dock alongside a huge freighter. Then the soldiers hurried the refugees out of the trucks and prodded them up the ship's gangplank. Some could barely move and were helped by those who could. The process was slow and the soldiers impatient. Col. Smith climbed out of his car and strode over to Roman. "Well, sir, here you are," he said, a thin-lipped smile easing his usual stern expression.

"Yes. Thank you," Roman nodded, stiffly, still at odds with everything. He looked up at the ship, made out its name, *Franz Ferdinand*. "That is Austrian registry?"

The British officer nodded. "The best we could do. We have been trying to secure passage for you for weeks."

"Where are we going?" Roman tried to match the officer's attempt to be friendly, but found it difficult.

"This ship will make many stops. But my understanding is that ultimately it will take you to Vladivostok."

"Vladivostok!" erupted Roman. "But that will put us right back in the hands of our enemies!"

The colonel shook his head. "No, I don't think so." Seeing Roman's anger rising, he held up a hand. "Please. Hear me out. We understand that the Red forces are far from Vladivostok and in serious difficulties with opposition from several different local governments in Siberia. There are also American and Japanese forces in and around Vladivostok. You will be quite safe, I can assure you."

"Besides" Col. Smith continued, "as you have probably heard, the Bolsheviks are not as interested in Siberia as they were in the other parts of Russia. Also, with the evacuation of your General Wrangel's forces from the Crimea, the Bolsheviks are apparently satisfied that you Whites are thoroughly defeated."

"But we are *not* defeated," Roman heatedly declared.

Col. Smith smiled. "I hope to God that you are not. I wish you well. Goodbye, sir." With that he turned and strode to his staff car.

Roman was unconvinced, but said nothing. The Bolsheviks were like a plague of locusts. They had one goal above all else: to make the former Imperial Russia, Bolshevik from Petrograd to Vladivostok,

Roman was convinced, the *Franz Ferdinand* was not taking them to safety, but back into the Bolshevik cataclysm from which they had recently fled.

Among the Caspian refugees, the other officers also refused to believe that they were being taken to Vladivostok. Repeatedly, angry voices were heard, "Why are we going to Vladivostok?" Even Roman was heard to say. "Is this the best the British can do; putting us on an old ship taking us back into all the horrors of the Civil War?" Finally, they decided that if they were taken to Vladivostok and saw a Red flag flying over the city, they would throw all the ship's crew overboard and sail to Japan. Still, many of the officers had heard that the revolution in Vladivostok was entirely different from the war in south Russia. Supposedly, the government there was opposed to Bolsheviks, thanks to the presence of Japanese troops. So, if there was a Red flag, it would signal that the Reds had conquered the last opposition in Vladivostok. But if they saw their national flag, the flag of St. Andrew, flying over the city they would know that the Japanese were still able to keep the Bolsheviks at bay.

No one could imagine how long this voyage aboard the *Franz Ferdinand* would last. What they didn't know, at first, was that they were not the ship's only cargo. There were also other refugees, on the ship.

Departing the great Basra harbor, the ship sailed through the Persian Gulf, out through the Strait of Hormuz and into the Arabian Sea and Indian Ocean. These places had only been names on a map to Roman, and had meant nothing at all to most of those in the Caspian group. Roman was able to keep a mental picture due to his quick mind and education.

They traveled onward, passing various Asian ports, stopping to load and unload cargoes. "Doesn't this ever end?" became a mantra.

In the humid heat, people crowded into any shady areas of the deck and welcomed the cooler nights. But, the weather changed drastically as they neared Japan: people now huddled together for warmth under a makeshift, hurriedly strung, tarpaulin that provided no shelter from the winds flowing across the deck. Some departed the freighter, claiming they would chance their lives to whatever community would take them; others had reached their end and died.

By the time the *Franz Ferdinand* approached Vladivostok, the group had dwindled considerably from the original four hundred refugees.

***

Finally, as the *Franz Ferdinand* plowed steadily northward, Roman's misgivings lessened somewhat. But, as they neared Vladivostok, he had new anxieties. This was late September 1921, already within winter's clutching grasp. They had been aboard the ship for many weeks; too long a voyage.

Troublesome thoughts discolored any elation Roman felt at the sight of land and this once distant city at last within reach. The health of those on board ship had deteriorated greatly. Could this forlorn outpost-like city care for these scores of refugees? Any kind of shelter would be better than this ship. Xenia, too, was a focus of his reflections. He had seen her only once, briefly, since the family reunion in 1918. He had no idea how she was faring, or even if she was still living. *Will we see each other again? Does she still love me? How can I find her?*

Pounding rain and piercing winds swept down from the hills that rose steeply along the ship's port side, seeming to crowd the ship in the narrowing passageway. As the ship steamed slowly around a bend in the coastline, the *Franz Ferdinand* finally came within sight of its destination. Vladivostok. What the refugees saw was a gray mass set against a gray background. Depressing—unlike the Russia they knew.

People crowded to the rails, peering into the distant indistinct city and unwelcoming atmosphere. Forlorn wooden and stone buildings stared back at them. Even their reluctant cheer was so faint it disappeared into the wind. What they sought was a flag—either Red or St. Andrew's—to signal what kind of life they would be discharged into.

Then came the first shout as the strongest eyes found it. "The Andrew's flag flies! The St. Andrew's flies!"

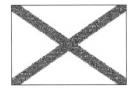

This flag with the light blue Cross of St. Andrew on a field of white was called "The Flag of Russia." It served as the Russian naval ensign for the Imperial Russian fleet.

Roman thought, *there is nothing gentle here*. But, then he saw the flag—the St. Andrews flag. It was the most gentle sight in this entire setting. Indeed, at this moment, it was the most inspiring sight he had ever seen.

The shout became a chorus, like a mighty sigh. That was the flag all had hoped for. Roman stood with several other officers amidst the crowd. *Yes! God is with us.* That was his initial thought. He looked at the officer next to him and nodded, getting an answering nod in reply. They had no words.

The city became more visible each minute, a bleak and unwelcoming blotch covering steep hillsides. Vladivostok hugged itself, seemingly trying to crawl into the hills for comfort. It was an outpost, the most distant point of the former Russian empire —or what had once been the empire—the nation's only port on the Pacific Ocean. Now it was merely a collection of structures, stacked steeply up the hillside, clapboard buildings built for hardy practical purposes not beauty. A few straggly trees braved the elements and clung to the weather-beaten soil, but they seemed utilitarian, also. There were a few old Russian naval ships.

As the ship drew closer to the inner harbor, the passengers could see a small group of men clustered on one of the docks. This appeared to be one small sign of welcome, at least. The ship's booming whistle shattered the clamped-down atmosphere and shook loose another shout from everyone on deck. As if to spite the climate and the city's dull spirit, the shipboard group's enthusiasm clearly declared they were glad to be land-bound again.

Men from the dock met Roman and superior officers with him at the bottom of the gangplank, smiling and shaking hands heartily.

The remnants of the Caspian Flotilla had finally reached their destination. How would they fare here? How long before they would be on the run again?

Chapter 29

Eighty officers and scores of seamen of the former Caspian Flotilla bolstered Vladivostok's inadequate navy and became the nucleus of the some 1,300 officers and men. Welcome as it was, this military strength was a far cry from what Vladivostok and Russia had once been. Roman learned just how far the city had fallen from its former state, from one of the men he met at the dock when they first arrived, an officer—like Roman—of the former Imperial Russian Navy. He was now a fugitive from the Bolsheviks.

"What you see," said the officer, "is only a miserable skeleton of what was Russia's major port on the Pacific Ocean. Once, before the revolution, we had a large military garrison here. We were the main base of our Pacific fleet! Even during the Great War, we were fine. The Allies, Britain and France, even Japan—and believe it or not, the United States—sent supplies through us to troops on the Eastern front, coming at Germany from behind. We had a great stockpile of supplies. The city was booming. We had good times. Life was as good as in many European cities about the same size as we."

Staring out over the harbor, the officer continued in a bitter tone, "What you see now is what the Bolsheviks have brought down on our heads." He turned to look up at the steep hillside above the dock area. "All that you see has come in the last three or four years. Under Kolchak, we had some hope of surviving, but the Bolsheviks killed him."

"This is the result of the Bolsheviks' promises: uncertainty, disorder and poverty. There's plenty of money, even a surplus—whatever the money is worth—but a terrible shortage of goods. We steal and plunder from each other just to stay alive."

Despairingly, he placed his hand on Roman's arm. "We are a shabby host. Forgive me—I should not burden you like this. We are delighted you have arrived. You are welcome reinforcements."

Roman understood the officer only too well. Other men had voiced feelings identical to Roman's own concerns. The man's words rang in his ears for a long time, increasing the heaviness in Roman's already burdened heart. Here in Vladivostok, he and Xenia were farther from each other than ever, and the chances of their ever seeing each other again grew slimmer by the day. He forced such thoughts from his mind by doing what he usually did, that is, pushing himself into the hardships of his new life.

The ships in Vladivostok's harbor—boasting of being its navy—were in wretched condition. They were actually far from being seaworthy in *any kind* of naval engagement. They had been cleaned and repaired, to the extent the local facilities allowed, by the naval newcomers. Some primitive dry-docks were built to hold a few of the ships while they were being worked on. Any extensive rehabilitation required weeks of effort in the frequently inclement weather. Eventually, though, the ships became what they were intended to be, a small but formidable navy, worthy of the title now bestowed upon it: The Siberian Flotilla, as it was called, was armed and supplied with sufficient ammunition and was in fighting shape. Yet, small as it was, it was considerably stronger than what the Bolsheviks bragged of—two five-ship squadrons based at the Bay of St. Olga and in the Tatar Strait.

***

Well into the winter of 1921, the Bolsheviks were harassing Vladivostok. They were more threatening than ever, but had not yet invaded the beleaguered city. Many held on to that thread of hope.

As more ships were repaired, Roman and his fellow newcomers were increasingly active in defending the area. More and more frequently, they found they were transporting White army forces and providing covering fire for landing parties as well as blockading Red-held ports. More often than desired, they were helping evacuate White troops from overwhelming Bolshevik forces.

The pattern of attack-and-retreat in the winter of 1921 and into 1922 was a repetition of similar skirmishes during the previous several years. But, now the intensity of Bolshevik pressure was heavier than ever, and skirmishes more frequent. Red forces always seemed to be at the city gates. To everyone it was clear: it was only a matter of time before the Revolution engulfed Siberia as it had all other Russian territory. A matter of time—but when?

No one could answer that, but preparations for evacuation began, with orders to be ready on a moment's notice to receive the city's population and put the Siberian Flotilla to sea. There was no other exit available. Vladivostok was a seaport. Escape had to be by sea. An inland route was a suicide journey into barren, largely uninhabited, or at best, sparsely inhabited frontier.

The one hopeful aspect of escape by sea was that the Red forces were nearing the city by land along the trans-Siberian railway. That frozen landscape, especially barren during winter made any progress slow and treacherous. It was the greatest of all obstacles to the Red advance and the greatest defense for Vladivostok.

Chapter 30

By early 1922, it was all too clear that the Bolsheviks had finally wiped out most of the White opposition. All that remained of any strength was in the far eastern reaches of Russia, beyond the vast expanse of Siberia, in the nation's only port on the Pacific Ocean—Vladivostok. The military strength there was growing weaker and unstable, subject to local political and tribal rivalries. To Roman, the reality was clear: Russia would never return to its former self. It had been plundered— for what? Most Russians had no idea.

Roman and Xenia had not heard from each other since the brief time they had enjoyed being together in Moscow in 1918. Each feared the other might be dead. Nearly four years was a long time to wait and hope. They had no idea of what had happened to the other. Had they waited for each other? That added to the despair.

Shortly after arriving in Vladivostok, Roman was slowly walking along the street when he was surprised to meet his aunt Georgia by chance. For the first time, he was hopeful that he might learn something about his family and possibly Xenia. He had seen her once before, in 1917, in Kharkov as he was changing trains on his return to Sevastopol following his visit to his father. The aunt had been a nurse aboard a medical evacuation train then. Now, he found out that she was living in Vladivostok and still medically treating wounded soldiers.

She was delighted to see him and told him. "Sadly, I know nothing about the family." When Roman told her about his desperation to know about his fiancée, Xenia, she said, "I have a doctor friend whose sister lives in Harbin. He has a lot of contacts and might learn Xenia's whereabouts since her father is well known. I'll ask him about her and the families." Roman expressed his gratitude and began to hope—despite the odds. With the chaos everywhere, mail service was unreliable and letters moved best and fastest by hand, from one friend to another.

Even though the aunt knew little, Roman grasped at every slight bit of news. He quickly wrote to Xenia, "What are you doing? Will you come?" For three or four weeks, he waited impatiently hoping. At last he received a short letter from Xenia. Her answer was. "I've worried about you. I'm with my parents in Moscow, but I have to work in a Bolshevik office. It's awful."

Roman savored every word even though she gave him only the barest of news. She asked more questions about him than telling about herself. "How are you? Are you healthy?

"Come. And come quickly," Roman replied by return letter through the contact. "I'm waiting for you."

Xenia replied, "I'll come. When? How?"

Roman hastily wrote, "Go first to the address of the doctor' sister in Harbin—but you must hurry because the Red forces are nearing Vladivostok. Don't tell *anyone* that you will be meeting a White in Vladivostok! It would be too dangerous."

Roman's letter took another three to four weeks. For him, the waiting time fluctuated between joy and anxiety. *Will she arrive in time? We might have to leave any day now.*

Xenia was determined to go. This time she persuaded her father to let her take the long and dangerous train trip; he had said "no" to their marriage for too long. Perhaps he sensed he wouldn't survive the year. He was both discouraged and in poor health and Xenia could no longer help him. When he encouraged her to go, she informed Roman by mail that she was coming and making preparations. Even so, she could not quell her nagging anxieties. Horror stories were repeated about Siberia and the dangers of the 6,000 mile train trip into the unfamiliar land.

At last Xenia took her fears and the letter to Father Mikhail, whom she trusted. But, before she even said anything, the priest looked at the rapt expression on her face and said, "You've had a letter." When she nodded, he said simply, "Go. You will be with him."

He didn't need to say more. He blessed her as she left, her determination flaming greater than ever and her fears surprisingly lessened. *I will go.* To Roman she wrote, "I'm preparing to come."

Still, the Bolsheviks' delaying tactics cost her four months. Finally, through a contrived story that she was going to Harbin, she gained permission to depart.

After saying her final, painful, goodbyes to her family, Xenia set out at last on the perilous journey across Siberia. She doubted she would ever see her family again and she prayed Roman was still there. *What will I do if he is gone?*

The Moscow train station was a daunting unkempt scene, but Xenia was too excited to care. Throngs of people rudely crowded, pushed, and moved in every direction They arrived on trains and left on others, struggling to find their next train, hoping there would even be a train. The service was still erratic. Soldiers in ragged uniform—no longer serving in any unit—hoped to get home. Children cried, hungry, holding on to relatives.

Any train trip took days under conditions that were unimaginably chaotic and frightening. Fighting was frequent along the railroad and trains often carried troops and armored cars. It was no different on Xenia's train. The erratic scraping sound of the train stopping and starting reinforced Xenia's fear that Red soldiers would question her. She feared another time of interrogation. Those memories kept her quiet and unobtrusive.

Recently, Xenia had heard that her dear friend Kira, Roman's sister, had been banished to the wasteland of Siberia sometime in mid-March, 1921. She, along with numerous other people had been exiled there because of political activities. She also learned that Kira had previously married and had a small daughter who had mysteriously disappeared.

As the train moved slowly toward the distant destination, Xenia saw the terrible disrepair and destruction of the beloved Russian *dachas*, or summer homes. Weeds had overtaken the once proud country gardens. She sadly endured the long, uncomfortable trip toward Harbin. Even Russia's famous white birch trees forests were mangled from the fighting. As the train moved farther east, the cold weather became more extreme and the previously luxurious trains no longer provided warmth. The once sparkling window by her seat was mud streaked and the metal trim rusty. She huddled under a blanket trying to keep warm and guard her two meager bags which allowed her to remain unobtrusive. She didn't dare attract attention to herself, so she avoided looking anyone directly in the eyes. She feared what might happen. Whenever she heard Reds talking, she struggled to keep from gasping for air.

Xenia was not beyond appreciating the stark beauty of the long trip despite the terrible destruction of her once proud country. Snow covered the land with a backdrop of the leafless birch trees and many frozen rivers. The train route around Lake Baikal was magnificent. It, the oldest and deepest freshwater lake in the world, curved almost 400 mile through south-eastern Siberia, north of the Mongolian border. *Such beauty*, she thought. *How did our country change into such a terrible mess?*

At last Xenia reached Harbin, China. It was known as a "Pink" city because there were zealous Red and White sympathizers (and many views in between) hopefully fleeing the war scene. It was a city of various cultures and it was also known as a city where you could find anyone.

When the train reached Harbin, Xenia nervously departed with her bags into unfamiliar territory. She cautiously observed her surroundings in this "wild" city as she sought the address of the doctor's sister. At last she found it. With her help and the help of others, she learned of Roman's whereabouts and quickly departed—just in time—for the next train.

As she left for Vladivostok, she was hopeful. Fears, however, continued to haunt Xenia, particularly because of the many stares of soldiers and the curious attention from people around her. She was not like most others traveling; they were poor, peasants, shaggily dressed and weary. Her clothing was less tattered, and she was alone; those appearances, especially, made her an object of curiosity. Her anxieties heightened as she tensely waited for the train to move. She overheard snatches of conversation, rumors, to be sure, that Bolshevik armies were closing in on Vladivostok. What she heard added to her worries. More and more Xenia worried. *Will Roman still be in Vladivostok when I arrive? Or will I miss him because the Red troops have driven them out? What then?* She could neither verify nor deny the truth of the conversations she overheard. She dared not ask; she felt mentally paralyzed,

Xenia's hope was fueled by the fact that Vladivostok, only a few hundred miles away now—about 500 miles—was very close, considering how far she had already traveled. But the waiting seemed interminable. She prayed constantly while trying to seem calm in spite of the turmoil.

At last the train began to move. Her hopes lifted immediately—until she heard another nearby conversation that sent dread through her. This supposedly was to be the last train allowed through to Vladivostok!

Again, anxieties overwhelmed her. However, the train kept moving, slowly at first through Harbin, then faster through the empty land beyond toward Vladivostok, the last outpost. She pretended sleep, but cautiously listened and wondered. *Will I be there in time? What will Roman look like? Will he be thin and haggard like so many of those around her?*

Eventually the train began to slow. She peered out the dirty window and saw homes, buildings, and disarray. A gray atmosphere blanketed everything. This had to be Vladivostok. Finally, she was here! At last. *Let Roman still be here! Lord God, please! Let the rumors of their departure be false.*

Xenia had the address of Roman's aunt which meant nothing to her at this moment. She knew nothing of the city. Fortunately someone directed her to the right street. As she slowly made her way through the slushy, dirty snow, she was terrified. She had started the process in the spring and now, she'd finally arrived at the aunt's on October 11, 1922, carrying with her only meager belongings and some precious pictures.

Taking a quieting breath, she knocked on the door. It was opened by a kindly-looking, middle-aged woman. "Xenia?"

Her eyes reflecting her concern, she nodded, then questioned, "Am I in time?"

The aunt's instant smile calmed Xenia's nervousness as the aunt quickly invited her in and gave her a big hug. "I heard the ships are preparing to leave. I'll go see what I can find out."

She was not gone long, but to Xenia it seemed endless as she waited. She was too nervous to sit still. Suddenly the door flew open and there was Roman. Tearfully they came face to face for the first time in years, finding themselves momentarily shy.

Joy was mirrored in Roman's warm, brown eyes as he quickly embraced her.

"You made it in time! You're safe. Thank God! I was afraid you wouldn't make it." Not meaning to scare her, Roman continued, "The Reds have reached the city. and we have to leave quickly. For us, the Russian Revolution is over."

As for Xenia, she barely recognized Roman. She had waited so long for this moment. *Am I ready for this? Has he always been so large?* As soon as she could, she went into the bedroom and cried.

Part Two:

A New World

Roman and Xenia

Chapter 31

In a simple ceremony devoid of friends and family except the aunt, Roman and Xenia were married the following day by a local priest early on October 12, 1922. There was little time for celebration after the priest blessed them and said, "I now pronounce you man and wife." Roman beamed and told Xenia, "I love you, but I don't know what is ahead for us." After a brief celebration, they boarded Roman's ship in preparation for departure.

By now, Xenia had gotten over her hesitation and was excited to finally be with Roman and under his protection. She bravely accepted it when he told her, "We need to prepare for a hasty departure."

Roman's gunboat was one of the first of the eight decrepit, vintage ships that pulled up anchors the next day and made haste for the open sea beyond Vladivostok's harbor. Some eight hundred refugees crowded onto the ships fleeing from the grasp of the Bolshevik troops invading the city only a few steps behind them. The last of the fifteen evacuating ships left October 24, 1922. Destination unknown. Future uncertain.

Amid uncontrolled tears and sad hand-waving, the passengers all felt similar pain: they were saying goodbye to their homeland and families. The tattered remains of the once-proudly hailed Imperial Russian Navy was now simply the last remains of the Russian flotilla which became known as Admiral Stark's Flotilla.

What fate awaited them? A watery grave? A new place to call home? They had all been forced to escape from their towns and homes. Now they were refugees trusting old ships. In a sense, *evicted* from *everything* they had ever held dear.

Roman and Xenia crowded with the others at the railing of his patrol boat. The tears and sadness were immeasurable. They were all seeing everything familiar fade into the distance. Fear, along with pain, was like a mask on everyone's face. Their lives, their country, and their families would never be the same.

Roman hadn't even been able to say goodbye to his family—didn't even know who was alive. Standing by Xenia as their homeland faded he said, "Xenia, it is only you and I now. We must be strong."

Roman's long-time dream of becoming a naval attaché came to an abrupt end. In the violence of the revolution, his dreams had vanished. Neither spoke for a long time, each caught up in their own tumult of emotions. They had been married only hours ago and were together at last. Xenia had overcome her hesitation and, like Roman, felt an indescribable joy at being with him. She was determined to have a happy marriage.

Vladivostok, the port from which Admiral Stark's Flotilla departed Russia

(From Wikipedia)

***

Fifteen days later, on October 27th, Xenia spent her twenty-fourth birthday aboard ship on a rolling sea in a totally foreign atmosphere trying not to mourn the loss of her own dreams: they were dead. Uncertainty about their future prevailed in their constant thoughts. The question of when would they return—if ever—to their homeland dominated the thinking of everyone in Admiral Stark's Flotilla. Yet, the Bolshevik fear was behind them—not fully understood. For so many of the refugees, active participation in the revolution was over or dramatically altered. They had all fled with only what they could carry. Xenia escaped with her beloved diary and few other treasures. Roman had already lost his treasures years before with the sinking of the *Empress Maria*.

Endless days. Growing monotony in cramped quarters. Constant white-frothed swells rendezvousing in the distance with the vast blue-gray sky were the daily backdrop of existence. Rationed food. Foul smells. Rolling stomachs. From sunrise to sunset, tumultuous seas tossed the ships from trough to trough in a never-ending, nauseating rhythm creating an ever-present danger. A typhoon destroyed two of the ships and all hands lost to the sea.

There was a sense of impermanence, but there was also the hope that some country would accept them. The first port of call was Gensan, North Korea, where most of the surviving ships and their evacuees remained for a period of repair and rehabilitation. A few refugees had elected to be left off in Japan.

More of the refugees were lost on the voyage from Korea to Shanghai. The remaining ships of the flotilla sought food, water, and essentials in Shanghai and more of the refugees chose to remain. However, the Chinese government did not welcome the aging, rusting ships so they were sent once again into the raging sea. The remaining refugees placed their fragile hope on acceptance at one other port, Manila, more distant but more promising. That city was now a territory of the United States—and was their last hope. The survivors all knew they wouldn't survive if they weren't accepted there. They continued on with conditions the same as before.

***

A unified shout erupted, "Land!" A small, tadpole-shaped island in the middle of a vast bay, Corregidor, southwest of the Bataan Peninsula, introduced the flotilla to Manila's huge harbor. In early times, fishermen and pirates had inhabited this volcanic island with its lush and abundant greenery and could easily launch unexpected attacks on those who dared to enter the Bay. Corregidor, approximately 30 miles west of Manila rose about 450 feet above sea level, had long remained a strategic outpost.

Wooded hills came into vision, and as Roman looked the other way—plains and rice fields were visible. But, the great elusive city of Manila—their city of hope—remained out of sight some thirty miles beyond.

Prayers were on the hearts of the survivors as they wondered, *Will they accept us? This is as far as we can go...*

***

"There it is!"

The remainder of Admiral Stark's rag-tag flotilla had arrived in the Philippines, at Mariveles on the Bataan peninsula. It was a hot, humid, and rainless January 29, 1923, with only the breezes to cool the remainder of bedraggled refugees.

Lacking passports and owning few personal treasures, the flotilla refugees fearfully, and hopefully, awaited word that acceptance here would end their wandering. In this new land—a land of drastically different climate and extremely different customs—they placed their revived faith.

Apprehension soared at first view of Manila's waterfront and harbor. Beyond, they saw skyscrapers and modern buildings against a backdrop of jungle foliage, palm trees and *nipa* (bamboo) huts which loomed on the horizon. A foreign land. No onion-shaped domes were visible. But, at day's end one of Manila Bay's spectacular sunsets brought with it a promise of a new day. Many wondered, *How long before we can return home to our beloved Russia?*

Holding back futile tears, Xenia sought refuge in Roman's arms. "It's so different. It doesn't look anything like home," she cried.

Most of those aboard the flotilla didn't realize how unique a city Manila was in Asia. It had been known, from medieval times until 1898, as a European-style fortified city. They saw the 16th-century massive walls surrounding an area known as Intramuros (meaning "inside the walls"). Churches, palaces, schools and wealthy homes inside these walls had been protected at times from naval invaders.

Finally, the Sturmers and the others entered that area through the beautiful, arched entrance for the first time, amazed at the combination of architectural styles surrounding them. With the arrival of the Americans, in 1898, after the Philippine independence from Spain, new architectural structures and government houses appeared. Some structures resembled Greek or Roman temples which blended with the beautiful Spanish architecture of such landmarks as the Roman Catholic Cathedral and Asia's first university, Santo Tomás University founded in 1611. Roman and Xenia were quick to observe and appreciate such contrasts in all the urban communities; the old mixed with the new, the magnificent mixed with the simple.

Weeks after their anxious arrival in Manila, a colony of the United States, General Leonard Wood, the U.S. governor-general of the Philippines, asked the refugees, "Who of you wants to go on to America?"

Many chose to take advantage of the safe passage arranged to San Francisco aboard the American transport, *Merritt*. They set sail in May as the season of heavy rains was just beginning. They had heard of the wonders of America and were excited at the opportunity to see it. It represented a land of promise.

"It is wonderful. General Wood! Oh, God bless him." exclaimed Roman to Xenia. "Can you believe he loaded about 500 of ours on a transport—without passport, money or permission—and is shipping them to San Francisco?" No law had been passed preventing this.

The Sturmers and a few others of their compatriots chose to remain in Manila, taking their chances. Xenia, by now expecting their first child, was unable to travel. *But, what will we do in this foreign country?* she wondered.

Chapter 32

The small Russian community looked forward to a fresh start and hoped a peaceful life awaited them. Most found the Philippines to be a land of warm breezes and heavy rains (during the two monsoon seasons), occasional typhoons, and friendly, industrious people. Loss of family and dreams of homeland were set aside as they focused all their efforts into adjusting and finding a means of support.

Dreams of naval ships, towering Orthodox churches with formal traditions, and pampered treatment were just that—dreams. Practicality was a necessity. A number from the flotilla became Philippine citizens. They could no longer go home and were not able to communicate with family or anyone in Russia.

Roman assured Xenia "I'm fortunate that I have my languages and should be able to find something." His working knowledge of languages—Russian, English, French, German, Polish, and Latin— provided him with an opportunity to teach. He sought the help of the French consul and became a professor of languages, primarily teaching French, at the beautiful Santo Tomás University. Roman also studied and learned to speak Spanish. Private tutoring supplemented their income.

***

"We have a baby girl!" Joy filled Roman's and Xenia's hearts when little Natasha Romanovna Sturmer— soon to be known as "Natalie"—was born on July 16, 1923 in Olongapo, Philippines. Xenia quickly set about making a new home for the little family and in a short while, as was her character, she also became an active part of the community. She was not one to sit still.

In 1927 with a growing student population, Santo Tomás University moved to a different location. Large expanses of lawn, an *arc de triomphe* and two circular fountains were infront of the growing campus. A medieval-looking structure topped by a huge clock tower stood at the far end along with many statues of famous people. It was there in the heart of Manila that Roman taught for a number of years. His knowledge of languages made it possible.

Roman eventually had an opportunity to become assistant sales manager of the Radio Corporation of America (RCA). Working for RCA, and also Zenith, selling radios and musical instruments, he earned more than as a professor. So he quit teaching French, although he never liked selling. It reminded him of selling the curling irons, but he tried not to think about the past. Roman had to play so many classical records for his prospective customers that soon he and Xenia became very knowledgeable about classical music. It became an important part of their life.

As president of the Russian refugee group, Roman helped other refugees get jobs. He sold many radios to government officials and, because of his job-getting abilities, he was able to help others as well as himself. He became known as far as Shanghai. This led to another activity—aiding stowaways escaping from China. Sometimes stowaways would sneak off ships and make their way to the Sturmer home. They'd then sleep, hidden in the Sturmers' large Willy's-Overland car parked in the garage. One time Roman was entertaining a former Cossack officer and offered to take him home. When they entered the garage, however, they discovered a stowaway who acted like he had a right to be there and refused to leave when requested.

"I will not!" he cried.

The officer reached in and forcefully lifted the man out. The irate stowaway then found a large rock and clouted the officer's head. So much blood was pouring down the officer's head that medical attention was needed. The doctor called the police and all three were arrested! It was the stowaway who was unfortunate enough to spend the night in jail—but not before he accused Roman, in front of the judge, of arranging the disposal of the flotilla ships and pocketing the money.

The judge asked, "Is that true?"

Roman was indignant. "No, it isn't", Roman firmly replied, informing the judge that the money Admiral Stark had obtained from the aging ships had gone to the Red Cross to aid some of the refugees. That was the last heard of that.

Xenia, Natalie, and Alex
in Philippines

Chapter 33

Roman continued to struggle finding his niche. He wasn't content. He missed the sea. In addition to the other sales, he also sold life insurance and managed an agency for radio receiving sets. Then he started his own business— importing goods from the United States. Life was good. And he still weighed in at a hefty 285 pounds!

In the early 1930's, Roman said to Xenia, "The Russian Orthodox Church needs a building of its own, even though we use one of the other small Christian churches. It is an important part of our lives. It was in Russia and is important to us as a family." Xenia agreed and said, "We need to pray for a church—and a priest." Although settled into Philippine life, far from Russia, their religious Russian heritage was never forgotten.

Following the local custom, they shopped daily in the market and bought what was on sale. But, at home, the food was generally prepared in the familiar Russian style. This pattern continued for many years. Food and special occasions were still a tradition.

On September 5, 1931 in that transition month when weather changed and drenching rain began to taper off, Alexis "Alex" Roman Sturmer made his debut into the world. Natalie was eight and joyfully became a big sister to him. The family had now grown to four. Roman happily announced to everyone he saw, "We have a boy!"

As expected, Natalie and Alex were both raised in the Orthodox Church faith. Education, also, remained extremely important to the Sturmers. As soon as Natalie was old enough, she was enrolled in the American School in Manila. She became proficient in reading, writing and speaking perfect English as well as Russian. At the time, no one had any idea how valuable these skills would be—skills that later would be a major factor in saving the Sturmers' lives.

A rambunctious Alex attended Letran Catholic School. Like all children, his curiosity got him into unpredictable situations. One time a terrified Xenia had to rush him to the hospital with scissors sticking out of his chest from a fall he had taken at school!

In 1935, a prayer was answered. A Russian priest came to Manila for the first time. Eventually a small wooden Orthodox church was built with a little entrance room that extended into the main part of the church. On the same lot, directly behind the church was the parsonage for the priest. It was a typical wooden house with a living room, a kitchen and several bedrooms. The priest asked Roman, "Would you be the choir director, psalm reader, and the first deacon?"

Roman happily accepted the priest's request and was excited to be an integral part of establishing the new church. He was proud to have the responsibility. This continued for the next ten years. Young Alex liked to wander around the church and naturally into places he was not supposed to go. One time he followed the bishop through the Royal Doors of the church (a no-no) and the bishop commented, "Someday, he will be a priest."

Gaiety and parties were prevalent in Manila. The vivacious Xenia

was never still unless she was reading—a passion of hers. Utilizing the training from her childhood ballet and theater, the diminutive Xenia started her own dance studio, or "school of physical culture" as she called it. There had always been much music in her own family. In fact, she had been told one of her grandmothers had been a concert pianist. She thought it was probably on the Harvey family side.

Xenia also organized numerous ballet performances for the benefit of the Russian War Invalids Society. Much to Natalie's chagrin, she had to play the male lead because of her height—five feet six inches—and slender build. Xenia herself loved to play the *femme fatale!*

Roman and Xenia were now earning enough to live quite well. They had their own frame house with a wide porch and wooden steps leading up to it. It was in this home that Xenia taught her "students of culture". She enjoyed that far more than cooking! It was not unusual to have Natalie or Roman do the cooking. "I'm busy with my school. Would you fix something? Or should we go out to eat?" Xenia enjoyed socializing.

Life was peaceful.

***

As she grew older, Natalie enjoyed going to school dances, but her father watched her like a hawk. Roman would question her thoroughly to make sure none of those "lecherous young bucks" had taken advantage of her! Roman told her, "I don't trust young men in the company of young women. After all, I was young once!"

But, Natalie had a mind of her own and wasn't so easily dominated by her father. She showed no interest in politics despite Roman's political leanings as he became more involved in local affairs. He became known as having very strong convictions.

Attempting to control Natalie, Roman used to drive her to the junior college and drop her off. But Natalie met and fell in love with an American serviceman of Polish heritage when she was a senior in high school. Determined to escape her father's strict control, she secretly married Edmund "Eddie" Alexandrowicz against her parents' wishes. What Roman didn't know was that Natalie would then go to the apartment where her husband lived after Roman left her off at school!

Xenia learned of the marriage, but managed to keep it secret from Roman. She was afraid of his reaction. He hadn't even been cordial to

Eddie when he met him. Natalie eventually got caught, but sadly, she only lived with Eddie for two short months.

Chapter 34

In December 1941, the Sturmers dreams shattered. The peaceful and profitable life everyone had known for eighteen years changed drastically once again. Disaster and terror first hit Pearl Harbor in Hawaii on December 7, 1941.

It wasn't long before everyone in and around Manila knew that Japan had declared war on the United States and rumors were reported that the Hawaiian Islands were completely destroyed.

On December 8, 1941 Alex was getting ready to go to school when he heard planes overhead. At age ten he was curious, so he ran outside and saw a sky filled with airplanes flying in formation obviously to some destination. He and several of his school friends didn't realize what was happening, until all of a sudden, bombs started falling all around the City of Manila. This was something new to them and they thought it exciting until the general public who'd gathered around them went into a state of panic.

"We're being bombed. Oh, my God!" screamed people on all sides.

Confusion reigned. The children didn't know what to do. They ran on to school, but when they got there, they were instructed to leave immediately. "Go to your homes quickly. Go directly and don't linger!"

Christmas Day, 1941, was one of the bleakest holidays in Philippine history. No voices singing carols, no holiday traditions and no exchanging of gifts. No special foods lovingly prepared. Everyone realized a full Japanese attack, like the one on Pearl Harbor, was eminent and they feared the actual invasion.

The fear became a reality when Japanese troops first marched into the southern outskirts of Manila on January 2, 1942 proclaiming control the same day. American sovereignty came to an end. Martial law was immediately imposed in occupied areas turning life upside down.

Little time elapsed before the Japanese Troops completely occupied the city. But, before it happened, the American forces destroyed all vital military installations including oil dumps by exploding them into oblivion.

Fire from the explosions lit the night sky. Debris—parts of buildings, roofs, lumber and bushes, branches from trees and so forth—filtered to the ground. Daytime brought more of the same, except the sky was now filled with darkness from the burning oil. Constant movement of trucks and equipment loaded with American troops filled all the main roads leaving the city.

There was much controversy over America's unpreparedness and lack of information that allowed the Japanese to land unopposed on Luzon Island. Nevertheless, it happened. Once again, war surrounded Roman's and Xenia's lives.

"I thought we were safe here. How can this be happening? What do we do? " Xenia cried out to Roman the day the Japanese marched in. His firm response was, "We must be wise and stay out of sight as much as possible without attracting attention. What else can we do?"

As General Douglas MacArthur withdrew his troops, Eddie, Natalie's husband was one of the first to join them. That night he came back to say his good-byes. The Sturmers were gathered in Natalie's large second-floor apartment weeping and hugging as Eddie gave a last look at Natalie and quickly left. Alex was instructed to keep out of sight, but watch from the large window which faced the front near the street's well-lit corner. "Oh, no," Alex whispered as some Japanese came into view looking over a map. "There are Japanese down there. They are hesitating…now they are speeding away. I don't think they saw Eddie's jeep parked in the shadows." With that, Alex breathed a sigh of relief. However, they were to soon learn that Eddie had been unable to get away. He was captured by the Japanese.

Within the next few days, Manila was fully occupied by Japanese troops issuing orders to the population to register. All captured

Americans were taken to concentration camps such as the one set up Santo Tomás University. As the other islands fell, camps were set up in those areas as well.

The Japanese didn't know the difference between White Russians and Red Russians; they just assumed that since Russia was not at war with Japan, they were allowed to live "normally", although they were closely watched.

Filipino and American soldiers were defeated, finally, on Bataan. They held out for three months. There is no accurate record, but estimates were that at least 10,000 men died of disease, malnutrition, thirst and brutality on the Bataan Death March of 1942. Compassionate Filipinos along the route tried to offer water, rice, and sugar to the prisoners and were rewarded by being burned alive by the Japanese.

Natalie grieved as she saw her husband—in the Bataan Death March—as the survivors marched through Manila in July. From a window of the apartment, the family watched Eddie struggle in that terrible trek to Bilibid Prison where he died there of dysentery. She had seen Eddie for the last time He didn't even know that as he was marched through Manila on that July day, Natalie had already given birth to Anastasia on July 1st. She would become known as "Tassy".

But before Eddie died, Natalie got word to him in Bilibid Prison by a Filipino friend of Xenia's—an electrician who worked in the prison—that he now had a little daughter. Hope of his survival was now gone.

A few weeks after the Bataan Death March, the Sturmers moved to an area outside of Manila, called Pandacan, where the Russian Orthodox Church was located. During the chaos their priest, who resided in the home next to the church, got frightened and moved out of the house and into the city leaving the church and its valuables abandoned. Roman, being close to the church, decided they should move there.

The Japanese occupation was filled with continuous experiences which the youth had to endure—and couldn't forget. School during the occupation was not different, except they had to learn the Japanese language and daily were exposed to the horrors of war. The Catholic school which Alex attended had very strict discipline imposed on them and every time they passed or came upon any Japanese soldier, officer or otherwise, they had to bow from the waist down. They also had to greet them in Japanese and have their papers checked. If anyone tried to by-pass any soldier or officer and were caught, the individual was slapped several times as punishment and sometimes was taken to Bilibid Prison where he or she went through a form of torture. The Japanese considered this just discipline.

Alex and Natalie now knew what it was like to live under a reign of terror, just as their parents had in Russia.

Throughout much of World War II, the Sturmers were treated officially as Philippine citizens and Russians of no-threat, but they had to endure polite or subtle cruelties themselves while witnessing others become victims of the atrocities of war. Like everyone else, they had to register. But, since the local Russian community was so small and, *supposedly*, the Russians were Allies in the Japanese eyes, none were put into prison.

Roman continually worried about the family and told Xenia, one day, "I heard that Anna returned home today to find her stepmother and son dead, bayoneted by Japanese soldiers." Xenia gasped and Roman held her as the tears began to flow. "We must be very careful."

During the first part of the war, food items remained basically the same, if you had money to pay for them.

The jungle interior of the Philippines provided cover for the many Filipino and American guerilla strongholds who continued to operate along strict military lines. Resistance movements transmitted from underground radios as the struggle continued for eventual freedom.

Barefoot groups with traditional weapons of bolos and bows and arrows fought; Catholics and Muslim Moros, regardless of religion or ethnicity. Most Filipinos believed in Douglas MacArthur's, "I shall return." And, in spite of the Japanese rule and brutality, most tried to help one another in whatever way they could despite the danger to themselves.

With his radio experience and desire for freedom, Roman never openly admitted that he was assisting, or was part of this underground movement, but from time to time there was speculation. He was very careful to monitor his actions as there were always informants.

Roman worked out a process to make boxes—match, cigar, shoe, etc.—using the bud leaves of the palm tree. Boxes were badly needed at that time and he continued supporting his family by manufacturing them in spite of Japanese opposition against his business. However, one day his factory mysteriously caught fire and burned to the ground. That was the end of that endeavor.

At that point, Roman and Xenia secretly hastened to make plans for their survival. "We have to be prepared," he told Xenia. "Look what happened in Russia."

J & P Oliver

Chapter 35

Natalie was compassionate and befriended some Russian girls who became prostitutes in order to survive. After becoming widowed, she had taught the girls English. They liked her and felt sorry for her, so they paid her enough money that she could provide a little food for the family. At this point, the family was barely escaping starvation. These same prostitutes urged her to enjoy the "good life"—like them —by getting a Japanese boyfriend. "No," she told them. I can't do that!" But, she still continued to help them and the money kept them alive.

Roman managed to move the family from their home into the Russian Orthodox Church parish house next to the church, where he had been a deacon. After the priest became frightened and abandoned it, Roman wanted to take care of the property and the valuables of his beloved church. After all, he had helped to establish it.

In the basement of the parish house, the Sturmers created a special hidden bomb shelter and it was there they and their friends hid many times. The family was advised that if any of the grenades, bombs, or anything else, would collapse the house, they would be killed, but they still hid there. Catastrophes were just waiting to happen with that refuge! It was the basement bathroom fixtures that finally destroyed their hiding place when a pipe broke..

Because they were White Russian, the Japanese still believed the Sturmers were not involved with the war in any way. They didn't know that the Sturmers were in the midst of it. They had Filipino friends who helped around the church. One big Filipino, Melchoir, especially liked Xenia and would often bring things to her. He was a thief who stole mostly possessions—pigs, money, and anything he could get his hands on—from the Japanese and bring it to Xenia to "save". She "saved" most of the things for Melchoir's wife, but much of the food that he shared kept the Sturmers alive. Then, one day Melchoir took one of Xenia's own chickens. She became very angry. "Melchoir, I trusted you! This is a big catastrophe; the eggs provide needed protein for little Tassy. Aren't you ashamed of yourself?" Melchoir just hung his head and promised not to do it again.

The Japanese motor pool was across the street from the parish house, so the Sturmers were witnesses, once again, to the many atrocities. For some reason, the Japanese were afraid of the Russians, so they didn't imprison them. Generally, they didn't bother them. But they were very hard on the Filipinos. If any Filipino was caught stealing, the employees of the motor pool were forced to surround the culprit and punish him until he went to "Filipino Heaven".

The Sturmer family had to quickly escape from the house so often on short notice that each member had a "special box" for some of their treasures. Xenia, Natalie, and Alex all kept diaries that meant a lot to them. When danger arose, the family tossed their boxes out the back windows before escaping into the brush and then—if there was time—they would go back for other things.

Often the family positioned themselves outside, hidden from view, where they could see the rice paddies. From their cover they saw Japanese soldiers firing on someone—probably Filipinos or Americans left behind—and heard the exchange of fire. Filipinos hiding throughout the paddies were so quick they would have the victims entirely stripped naked of their clothing and shoes before they hit the ground. Then the Filipinos would go hide in their *nipa* huts, the native homes made of bamboo.

Bamboo was tied together and covered with a roof of the nipa/anahaw leaves to make the huts, many of which were stilted. They were built in a clearing surrounded by coconut trees with some designs going back as far as the time of the Spaniards.

The Filipinos were proud of their huts and considered them an icon representing communal unity.

Daily activities were not always so grim. At times they were downright humorous.

An example of a jungle nipa hut.

One of Sturmers' neighbors who lived near the parish house needed help in butchering his pig because he didn't know how. Always ready to step in, Roman pretended he knew how to do it. The slippery pig kept running around and around and slipping from their grasp. By the time they killed it, the pig had so many knife wounds that he was already partially butchered.

The parish house was located at the end of a road—close to the Philippine Film Company. One day a Japanese officer questioned the family about a Filipino actress he wanted. He was *sure* she was in their house. He was so upset that he kept stomping on a board over the cesspool at the back of the house. Roman warned him, but he just kept ranting and stomping. The officer wanted that actress and wasn't going to give up. He didn't care that she was married, and that was that! One too many times he stomped. The rotten timbers gave way. The next thing the officer knew he was splashing around in excrement and trying to get out: but couldn't!

"What can we do, Dad? I'm not helping him. He stinks."

"We can't let him drown in there. We must be compassionate— even though he's our enemy."

"Okay, but I'm not getting near him."

Roman felt the same way, but they extended a wooden pole to the officer who grabbed it and was pulled out of the foul mess. Both Roman and Alex backed as far away as possible. The officer remained angry. When he didn't leave, they became frightened. He now insisted on searching the house!

Hoping to mislead the officer, Roman said, "If you think she's here, go ahead, and feel free to look." His ruse didn't work.

When they had first seen the officer, the rest of the family had taken refuge in the basement (not the usual hiding place) along with some other people—including the actress.

But, now, dripping, dirty and smelly, the angry Japanese led the way as Roman and Alex fearfully followed him into the basement. Everyone was forced to line up in a row as the foul-smelling officer repeatedly walked up and down. He kept looking, but he did not recognize the actress.

While Roman and Alex had been assisting the Japanese officer, quick-thinking Xenia had dressed the Filipino actress in some of Alex's clothes. The actress was so terrified that she turned stark white. Even Alex didn't recognize her. The family had a tough time keeping a straight face despite their fears. The officer thought she had gotten away, so he left. The Sturmers were then left to clean up the smelly mess.

Sometime after the actress incident, Roman and some others were ordered by a Japanese officer to go to the area known as San Diego for questioning. Few people—Filipino or whites—ever returned from there. The prospect was terrifying.

The officer, looking for Roman, came right into the parish house and impatiently ordered Roman to accompany him. Roman's feet were extremely swollen by now from beriberi. "I can't walk!" he insisted. The soldier finally agreed to leave without him and take Alex instead. Xenia was frantic and tried to distract him by asking questions. She discovered the soldier had been educated in the United States and spoke fluent English. Utilizing that knowledge, she was finally able to convince him to leave Alex.

Others were not so fortunate. Several of Roman's friends, Victor Charnetsky and George Ovsoff, from the Russian Navy, also lived in Manila,. One day Ovsoff came home to find his pregnant wife murdered for no reason. The Russians surmised that because guerrillas would sneak in and kill Japanese soldiers, the Japanese started to kill a number of townspeople in retaliation—children as well as adults. Their favorite method of torture was to put a hose in a person's mouth, turn on the water and then stomp on the stomach. One of Alex's young friends was killed this way.

Fear became a constant companion.

Who will be next?'

Chapter 36

The beautiful old university of Santo Tomás, that Spanish vestige from the 17th century, provided forced housing for thousands of Allied civilians who became prisoners. The courtyard was filled with shanties crowded together, scant protection for all the ill and dying people. The Americans in the prison tried to start schools, initiate authority for control, and start a clinic of sorts. But, hunger and malnutrition were rampant. Parents fed their meager rations to the children and became fleshless bones with swollen legs themselves: literally skeletons; ghosts of their former selves; many of whom never lived to see a better day.

As General Douglas MacArthur prepared to invade and reclaim Luzon, the burning of Manila began. The Japanese frantically set fire to everything they could. Retreating Japanese destroyed Manila's military installations, water supply, electric power system, and bridges. Beautiful historic landmarks were demolished.

Until American troops stormed Manila in February 1945, the White Russians were ignored. But, when the Japanese saw the end had come, they ordered all of them be rounded up. The Sturmers had been forewarned that the church and their house were going to be burned so they started salvaging and hiding all the books, icons, etc. they could.

When the Japanese set fire to the front porch of the church, Roman and Alex got a hose and put it out. Then fire was set to the back of the church. Again, they put it out.

Roman, Xenia, Alex, Natalie and little Tassy hid in the basement of the parish house until the Japanese came to set fire to it once again. The family had kept farm animals at one time and they still had a pig running around in the yard. Their first warning of this attack came when the Japanese threw a grenade at the parish house and it hit their pig instead. The explosion gave them a dire warning. But, one by one the Japanese lit gasoline rags and shoved into the basement. Fires were ignited throughout the night with Roman and Alex frantically kept trying to put them out.

As fire finally was consuming the whole house, the family managed to escape by crawling on their hands and knees through the tall grass and weeds behind the house just before the Japanese realized their victims had not perished.

With their home and church in the Pandacan area obliterated and most of their own personal treasures destroyed, the Sturmers survived by moving nearer the jungle and living under trees until they found a vacant *nipa* shack that hadn't been burned by the Japanese. Their new home had typical room dividers of capiz shells made from the outer shell of marine mollusks found in the shallow coastal waters of the Philippines. The open windows allowed cooling breezes in, but made mosquito netting a necessity at night.

Desperate for food, the family ate rice salvaged from the rice paddies around them, even though it was laden with big, drowned black ants. This rice, and rice salvaged from sunken Japanese ships bombed by the Americans, was their main staple. The oil and gasoline smell that lingered on the rice was very unpleasant. Even numerous washings didn't eliminate the odor—but it was available and cheap! It was food to keep them and their hope alive.

Xenia learned how to make stew from banana stalks and sometimes the ants even managed to get into it. Roman just said, "Well, we have meat."

The Sturmers became skin and bones. Once a hefty 285 pounds, Roman dropped to 140.

Alex had the chore of emptying the "honey pots", a necessity in a hut where no bathroom existed. He continually watched the American and Japanese war planes "dog-fighting" overhead. One day he, Roman, a friend, and "Sailor", Alex's dog, were jumping up and down with excitement on a cesspool cover that had been riddled with bullets as they watched the battles. They forgot where they were and, as in the case of the Japanese officer, the cover gave way and the four of them went swimming! Even the dog had to paddle. The remainder of the day was spent with a make-shift shower, trying desperately to scrub off the smell.

One time Japanese soldiers fired machine guns from the edge of a clearing, but the Sturmers had been warned and hid. The Japanese were afraid of the guerillas and advancing Americans so they retreated, forgetting their objective and didn't go further into the jungle.

As the sun was coming up one morning, Roman and Alex heard something not far from them. Roman had great difficulty, but they both managed to creep through the underbrush to find out what was happening. They wondered, *what awaits us?*

Roman whispered to his son, Alex, "Go one way and I will go the other and we'll meet at a bridge". To their joy, they heard English voices. As the G.I's talked, Roman and Alex realized the Japanese were gone. It was February, 1945, the beginning of the end of World War II.

The liberation of Manila and the other islands, however, was far from over. The resulting fires burned much of the northern part of Manila. Flames could be seen for fifty miles around. Mountain strongholds of Japanese and artillery caches made liberation an ugly, costly affair.

The Philippines national economy was devastated, as well as the physical aspects of the country. Poverty, black-marketeering, and disease existed everywhere. Many of the survivors in Santo Tomás were freed. But Manila and the surrounding country had died. In its sprawling ruins lay the bodies of more than 100,000 Filipinos who had perished during the battle for the city—at least six civilians for every fighting man killed on both sides.

Manila was a city of death. The smell of death permeated everything. Fires, slaughter, mutilation and rape were rampant by the enemy. Even underground shelters held those buried alive. The magnitude and lack of facilities made burial a major problem. People wandered around with no place to go. Freedom had been costly.

***

During this time of liberation, Natalie met a persistent suitor, Lt. Bert Hamel, an American soldier. He had been warned by an army buddy that Roman tended to be a little biased about some things and was pretty firm in his beliefs, but Natalie was more open. The first time Bert arranged to visit Natalie, Alex waited on the bridge to direct him. This was the same bridge where he and his father had first learned of the liberation.

Bert described the Sturmer shack to a buddy as "an elevated hut on stilts to remove it from the mud and pig shit." All the Filipino bamboo huts had pigs running under them and Bert had to wear his army boots when he started courting Natalie. It was March 1945 and their romance survived the mud, pigs, and huge sewer rats that scurried across the bamboo rafters in the *nipa* shack. One time Bert wanted to blast a rat to "rat heaven" with his 45 caliber pistol, but Natalie said, "No, I'd rather have the rat than the blood and guts all over the shack."

Natalie married Bert on August 11, 1945 in a wedding dress donated by the Red Cross, and they soon left with three-year-old Tassy for their new home in Berkeley, California.

Roman joined the American Army and worked in the Philippine Office of Censor because of his knowledge of the Philippine language. During this time the family continued living in the *nipa* shack

Xenia and Roman had been born to the elite, but they realized they would never have survived without diligence, discipline, dedication and frugality. It and the grace of God had carried them through.

After a brief time, as the Philippines began the long trek down the road to recovery, the Sturmers felt that God had once again favored them and allowed them to begin—anew—in the United States, thanks to Bert Hamel's paperwork on their behalf. The family missed being together, so they made a decision to leave Manila for yet another unfamiliar territory. They desired to see their new granddaughter, Katherine, born to Bert and Natalie in 1946.

With their meager possessions, and a few treasures—including one icon they salvaged from their beloved church—the Sturmers stepped on board a converted freighter named *Golden City* headed for the West Coast of the United States. Optimism and an appreciation of their daily blessings abounded. Once again their personal treasures had been destroyed, but they still had each other and the bond was strong.

Part Three:

Interlude

Chapter 37

California 1946

The USS *Golden City* docked in San Pedro early in 1946. She was a freighter, converted to a troop transport, and commissioned into the Navy in May 1944, returning veterans to the United States from the western Pacific. The Sturmers were among those departing after the long voyage. The rough seas made most of the few passengers sick—except Roman. He loved the food—and the sea. Xenia, in particular, gratefully exited the ship on her sea-legs. "I never thought I'd have to get on another ship again," she quipped, "but I can hardly wait to see the family...and another new home."

Roman and Alex were less vocal at first as they stepped ashore and saw a land very different from anything they had known before, but they had survived. And they would do so, again. Alex, an impatient teenager, vocalized their thoughts when he asked, "I've never been on a train before. How long before we get to Berkeley?"

Roman's only response was, "I don't know yet."

The Sturmers caught a train to Berkeley with little difficulty as they spoke English very well. Although it was April, the train had to stop to clear the tracks of snow and an excited Alex was allowed off the train to make his first snowball. *Everything is so clean and the weather is cold*, he thought. *And there's no sign of destruction. Was the snow like this in Russia for Mom and Dad?*

When the train pulled into the Oakland station, Natalie's face beamed as she spotted the rest of her family. The Hamels rushed to meet the train and be reunited once again with their family.

After the hugs, kisses and tears all around, Bert asked Roman, "How was the trip?" True to form, Roman gleefully declared, "Oh, my, we ate our way to California." With a big smile, Xenia quickly reached out to hold Tassy and baby Kathy. Alex concentrated on comparing the buildings to those in Manila.

Roman, Xenia, and Alex arrived in the San Francisco area with no immediate place to call "home". For a while, they lived with the Hamels and then moved to a one-bedroom apartment in a building on University Avenue in Berkeley. The industrious Xenia quickly noticed the apartment complex needed a manager and obtained the position of managing not only it, but the adjoining one as well.

The family began to make new adjustments. Roman was given the opportunity to work in a Heinz-57 cannery alongside his son-in-law, Bert. As was Roman's characteristic, he worked diligently on the cannery equipment and enjoyed the peace—but still he remained dissatisfied. *This work is a survival job necessary to provide for the family but I'd like something more challenging. What can I do with my education and fluency in language?* Daily the thoughts bombarded his mind as he went off to work.

Someone made a suggestion to Roman about looking into a teaching position at the Army Language School in Monterey, California. With nothing to lose, he pursued the possibility. Both his determination and his extensive knowledge of so many languages eventually provided Roman entré to the famed school in August, 1947. He was happy that he no longer had to work at the cannery and rejoiced that the teaching matched his abilities.

At the Army Language School's request, Roman wrote and developed a difficult 1,380 - hour course of Russian and trained the servicemen in the language and culture for the school. He easily settled into his new life and the challenging work.

Alex was almost fifteen, but he had no school records from the Philippines, so he first had to enroll in Garfield Elementary School in Berkeley. He quickly progressed to his correct level. Once he entered Berkeley High School, he worked part-time at a drug store and also a drive-in restaurant. He liked having money of his own and he'd already learned a good work ethic.

Because of the long round trip from Berkeley to Monterrey, it was necessary for Roman to remain all week at the language school; thus he became a week-end father to Alex—as strict with him as he had been with Natalie. One night Alex came home a little late and tried to sneak in. He carefully avoided the squeaky steps and fit his key very quietly into the lock. But was he safely in? No! He was not prepared for the sudden cuckooing of a clock—a new gift from the Hamels who were now stationed in Germany—and he reacted by knocking over a small stand by the door.

Suddenly Alex was greeted by his angry father. "What have you been doing? You are late!"

"I'm sorry, Dad, we just lost track of time." He had become a typical American teenager.

Roman, however, made it clear he was displeased. "Don't let it happen again." Alex simply responded, "Yes, sir," and went to bed.

Roman felt it was the man's position to make the decisions, and he truly was the patriarch. He still carried with him many of the traditions and customs of his homeland. Perhaps it was that quality that had brought the family through so many trials and tribulations.

In keeping with their heritage, family and church were pivotal points in their lives. They became active in St. John the Baptist Orthodox Church in Berkeley and were proud to be able to hang the large icon there which they had managed to salvage from their little church in Manila.

Roman soon became a deacon and Xenia became a reader. She also sang in the choir. It was here, in their new church home, that they developed many new friendships and maintained old ones with former Russian shipmates and their families. It was a happy, social time for them.

Alex graduated from high school in 1951, and felt called to serve what he now considered "his country". He joined the Marines in 1952, and was trained in "underwater demolition".

In February, 1954, shortly before his discharge, Alex met his future wife, Mildred "Millie" Wilson. In May they were married in the family church in Berkeley making it a "red-letter" (special) year for them, even though the couple moved to Southern California.

Millie affectionately called Alex's parents by their Russian nicknames, *Dedu* (Roman) and *Babu* (Xenia) and they always greeted her, and others, with a kiss as was the Russian custom. Although they didn't watch much television, both Roman and Xenia loved reading their many books, magazines and newspaper—often in languages other than English. They continued to listen to music as they had done in the Philippines.

The elder Sturmers were proud of their adopted country, even while adhering to many of the customs of their Russian heritage. They appreciated all that had been given them and they proudly hung a portrait of the President of the United States in their home. Xenia continued to love plays and ballets—and occasionally a drink with "no ice, please". Roman belonged to a Russian Naval Club. He loved talking with friends there he'd known for many years.

One evening after dinner, as they were quietly reading, Roman said to Xenia, "I'm planning on retiring from teaching. What do you think about me becoming a priest?"

Stunned, Xenia looked at Roman, and uttered one word, "Why?" She knew this was no sudden decision just as Roman knew Xenia would go along with his decision—although she would express her own thoughts.

"Alex got married this year and I've had two small heart attack scares. I want to do something of value with the rest of my life. I heard that the church needs English-speaking priests in Alaska and it set me to thinking. I think I've had a long-held desire tugging at my heart to become a priest."

Roman was very devout and had served in the church all his life. For years—in his time in the navy and in service for the Whites, then during the family's long tenure in the Philippines—he had helped the local priests in one way or another. Why had he always been led to do that? He knew they had been blessed and protected. Now in his fifties, a world away from the other lives he'd safely lived through, the desire blossomed into full fruit: He would become a priest himself. In some way, he would repay God for protecting him through those countless dangerous situations.

Xenia knew better than to argue. Anyway, it sounded like a good idea to her. "I understand they speak Russian there. I wonder if Kodiak has a good library?" She was already planning the move.

In late 1954, after much study and meeting the requirements to become a priest, the Primate of the Orthodox Church in North America named Roman Sturmer the Parish Priest of the Resurrection Church of Kodiak, Alaska. It had been easy for Roman having been part of the church for so many years. Now, Roman was Father Sturmer, a priest-missionary going to a land he'd never seen but knew continued many traditions from his own Russian heritage.

Xenia, being the loyal wife, began preparing for another move, a long one.

Roman retired from teaching in December, 1954, and received an outstanding commendation from Headquarters, Army Language School, Presidio of Monterey, California, for his seven years of service. In addition to teaching and writing at the school, he had also been Administrative Assistant in the Division.

Roman and Xenia packed and headed to Kodiak. Their children were now independent and it would just be the two of them together embarking on a new adventure.

Part Four:

The Homecoming

Kodiak, Alaska

Kodiak Island, Alaska, lying off the southwestern coast of the mainland, is Alaska's oldest and most historic European community, rich in Russian, Aleut, and Alutiiq Native traditions and culture. Heritage of early Russian explorers and fur traders along with a strong commercial fishing industry add a unique culture to the island.

The island was originally called "Kadyak" or "Kikhtak" from 1763 in keeping with the sound of the native Alutiiq word meaning " island". The name officially became Kodiak in 1901 because of common usage.

By 1793 the Russians had gained control over the natives as a result of trading and the Russians' weapons. The city of Kodiak was originally called "Pavlov Harbor" (Paul Harbor) by the Russians and was the center of the Russian government in Alaska until 1808 when they moved their capitol to Sitka. In approximately 1794 the Russian Orthodox clergy arrived in Kodiak in an initial attempt to convert Alaskan Natives to Christianity. They performed baptisms and marriages along with eventually establishing a school and orphanage. Conversion by coercion was forbidden by them. Lifestyle differences, language barriers, and shamanistic practices all had to be overcome. By the late 1800's other denominations began to arrive and establish missions. However, Russia's last remnant of their colony, the Orthodox Church, remained a dominant religion of the island villages and was a central feature of social life.

It is said that once some natives converted to Orthodoxy they often tried other denominations but many returned to the Orthodox formality.

Chapter 38

Only three hours from Seattle by air, Kodiak, the largest of the Kodiak Island archipelago, became Roman's and Xenia's new home here on the "emerald isle", which was surrounded by smaller islands and scenic fjord-like bays. They found a landscape carved by glacial retreat thousands of years ago and mostly lacking in foliage or small vegetation because of the volcanic soil. Roman would be the priest for this entire area which included six small villages on the 177 mile-long main island, in addition to the city of Kodiak.

The land of dreams, rugged wilderness, magnificent beauty, and permafrost opened its arms to Roman and Xenia on December 16, 1954. They arrived, ready and anxious, to serve people in the Kodiak region: a place where King Crab feeds were world renowned; fishing was the #1 occupation; and the *aurora borealis* performed a striking dance of colors through the skies. It was a region far different from California in all aspects; but it was also rich with familiar Russian characteristics that would quickly make them feel at home.

Xenia remarked to Roman upon arrival, "I knew the mid-winter days would be dark and short in contrast to the long, warm Alaskan summer nights, but I'm surprised the marine climate seems so temperate."

The mild weather allowed for many outdoor activities from bird watching to boating, and of course fishing. Father Roman found these interesting, but they didn't appeal to Xenia.

Wildlife and raw wilderness abounded in the archipelago: Kodiak brown bears, fox, mountain goats, deer; sea lions, whales, salmon, King Crab, halibut; and many species of birds including eagles, cormorants, and gulls. Otters loved to frolic in the waterways.

Seldom was there freezing weather, although frequent clouds and fog covered the area. Because this was located in one of the world's most productive fishing areas, necessary services—food, repairs, processing, etc.—brought in many fishing vessels to Kodiak from the Gulf of Alaska and the Bering Sea. Both commercial and subsistence level fishing played a major role on the islands, something new to the Sturmers as they had never seen it in Russia or their other homes.

Roman and Xenia could adapt easily to the language although it differed somewhat from theirs. Russian was still spoken by many, although there were few pure Russians remaining in Kodiak. The native tongue had a slightly different accent and they had added words to the vocabulary. Old-world customs existed on some of the islands side-by-side with the American flag which delighted the Sturmers.

The Russian Orthodox Church of Kodiak presented an impressive sight to Roman and Xenia. Built originally in 1794, in the same location on a small hill away from the waterfront, the church was a beautiful sight. Although three of the Russian Orthodox churches on that site had accidentally burned down, including one in 1943, many items, such as the original altar decorations and books were salvaged. Some of the articles in the church even dated back to its founding, including gifts to the church by Catherine the Great. The familiarity enhanced Roman's and Xenia's feeling of being at home. They had a purpose.

The church view that greeted them was that of a picturesque wooden whitewashed building with narrow-paned, bullet-shaped windows and a set of covered steps leading to the entrance. Two cupolas rested on top of the building at opposite ends. On these were vibrant blue "onion-shaped" domes topped by tall crosses, typically Russian.

Several evergreen trees flanked the side yard but nearby were some oil tanks. "I don't like those," Roman expressed with concern to Xenia. "They are dangerous and too close to us."

On the knoll away from the water were several other churches. Diagonally across the street from the church stood the parish house, the Sturmers' new residence. It was a century-old monument built mostly of cedar with little green scrolls adorning it, adding to the atmosphere of the region.

***

Disaster struck just four months after their arrival.

Early on the cold morning of April 9, 1956, the oil stove in the living room of the parish home burst into flame. The intense smoke awakened Roman. "Fire! The house is on fire!" he cried. "Help me get the fire out! No! Get out and yell for help! The phone is too hot! I can't call the fire department," Roman managed to yell from their back porch.

Awakened by Roman's screams, Xenia was able to escape and ran to the neighbors for help. Meanwhile, another neighbor heard the calls for help, saw the red glow and reported the fire. The fire department arrived quickly, but water pressure was so low on the hill that a pump truck was dispatched to the beach for additional water. Due to low tide, hoses had to extend about two thousand feet to provide the water in any helpful amount.

The old cedar house, tinder dry, quickly burned to the ground.

In the attempt to put out the fire and save important papers, Roman's right leg, hands, and back were so badly burned he had to be hospitalized. He also suffered severely from smoke inhalation. The injuries were severe enough that he required recuperation in the hospital for some time. Eventually he fully recovered.

Everything was lost—another episode of family losses. Everything the Sturmers had accumulated both before and after leaving the Philippines—books, a stamp collection, personal treasures—was gone. The ground near the oil tanks that Roman saw as a potential danger had been doused with enough water that they'd been prevented from catching on fire.

Father Roman Sturmer and Xenia

Chapter 39

The Kodiak Health Center became temporary housing quarters while a beautiful new home was built during the summer months by the parishioners for Father Sturmer and Xenia. One problem: since they built it, the parishioners assumed it was theirs and often just walked in—without an invitation. Xenia was sociable, as well as energetic, and did love to entertain—but so many people continually coming to their house was too much even for her. There was no privacy.

In the September 3, 1960 edition of the Kodiak Mirror newspaper, Father Sturmer commented on their many losses, "Since my mature life, I have stopped caring for personal belongings because, to begin with, my first ship blew up during the First World War and I lost everything. Whatever of ours did not burn in Manila, was finished here." He said the books and their hi-fi (high frequency audio system) were theirs and all else belonged to the church.

In the same issue of the Mirror, Xenia was credited with saying, "I like something nice, but if I lose it, I am not so upset; I lost everything in Moscow, and that time in the Philippines, and now in the fire here. I am used to it."

In addition to his many duties and necessary travels, Father Sturmer readily accumulated many other responsibilities. The article also credited him with saying, "I am some kind of real estate agent because the church owns lots of land in town given by Presidential decree to the Orthodox Church of America (years before) and I am a collector for leases of land."

In 1956, at age 60, Father Sturmer decided he needed to learn yet another language, Greek, so he did just that. With determination, he studied until he could both speak and write it fluently.   Xenia wondered, *What next!*

Before Father Sturmer arrived, not only had there been no priest in Kodiak, but there was no psalm reader at the church. Since Xenia had had equal experience in psalm reading, she became the psalm reader. After all, *Matushka* (wife of the priest) Xenia had been helping in that role since 1934," Roman told the parishioners. She had a gentle melodious singing voice and loved doing it. She also directed and sang in the choir and became the church secretary.

In addition to her regular church duties and her main role as a psalm reader, Xenia was a Hospital Auxiliary Grey Lady, a member of the Business and Professional Women's Club, and was the community librarian. She claimed to have read every book in the library. She still had high energy.

Roman was responsible for eight additional Orthodox churches on Kodiak Island and the Alaska Peninsula. Because of the distance involved and his many activities and commitments, Roman seldom got to visit them more than once a year. But, both he and Xenia particularly loved to go to Spruce Island to visit an old monk, Father Gersim. Roman declared to him, "You are a great cook." Nothing had changed; he still loved to eat!

Roman's daily routine as priest included a service at the church twice a day. He also liked to go grocery shopping—unless the weather was really bad. The Sturmers had a pattern. Xenia made out the grocery list and Roman went to the store, selected and paid for the groceries. And then he had them delivered. It was another opportunity for him to talk to the islanders, which he dearly loved to do.

The multi-tasked Roman *also* taught language classes at the military base, taught Bible School for his parishioners, edited and published the monthly church magazine, and was often sought out to be a speaker. He was also on local television quite often. Everyone knew him.

In April, 1958, the Sturmers invited Alex and Millie with their infant daughters, 6-week-old Laura and 18 month-old Karen, to live with them. Despite all their relationships and duties, Roman and Xenia missed family and wanted them nearby. Alex went to work at Bank of

Kodiak but didn't like it. After living in Kodiak for nine months, Alex and Millie decided to move back to California.

Millie expressed to Alex, "Papa loves Kodiak. He's a big fish in a little pond; he's involved in many things. He's an active member in the Rotary Club, the Toastmaster's Club, teaches Russian at the naval base and publishes a monthly church newspaper besides all the many activities related to the church."

She further mentioned to Alex that she was amazed when watching Roman in the living room of their home. "His desk sits in front of a window; he has the television on, his classical music is playing, and he's watching the people outside. He's also on the move—you don't dare leave a light on in the kitchen—or in any room—for he will be right behind turning off the light. How does he do it?"

And, of course, 8 o'clock was time for the nightly ritual of tea and cookies. The whole family took part.

Interior of Kodiak Church from a clipping 1950's

The Kodiak church is reputed to the first of its kind to
be found in the Western Hemisphere. There were 400
member of Father Sturmer's parish.

Chapter 40

Since Kodiak was a little bit of Russia existing in the far North, holidays and rituals were all-important. Everything from painting and exchanging gaudy Easter eggs to celebrating the many saints' days and eating the traditional Russian *pirojki* were part of tradition. For Roman and Xenia, it brought memories of their lost homeland closer to them.

Life on the islands was not easy for the natives. Fishing, the primary livelihood, was very dangerous, and many times boats would be found washed clean by the sea and the bodies never found. So many were killed as a result of fishing that families would have many children. The tenuousness of life may be one of the reasons that the many celebrations were so important.

One of the Sturmers' granddaughters, Kathy, Natalie's daughter, lived in Alaska with them on Kodiak in 1960 when she was about thirteen. The waterfront with all the boats and stores interested her. She liked to go there. This was where a drive-in, a post office, seven bars, twenty-four liquor stores, and one movie theater were located. The churches were located on higher ground, up a small hill away from temptation.

When the tide was out, there was a little inlet that Kathy and a friend could walk across to Near Island where seaplanes landed. There was a dry dock on the lower part of this island and on a raised area were a hospital and the Catholic Church.

Music in the Russian Orthodox Church is considered very beautiful and was composed by many famous composers primarily for the church. "But," Kathy wrote in a letter to her parents, "...in Kodiak, when the Aleutians come to church—to either service—and sing, their voices strongly ring out with an Asian overtone. I find the resulting music an interesting combination."

The one hour of darkness in summer and the less than one hour of sun in the winter made it difficult to tell the time. It also made summer-time sleeping an unusual situation.

Going to school in the dark of winter, the children had to follow a ravine until they saw the lights of the school…and when they returned it was also dark. Basketball was the big sport. But, often in the winter kids could swim in the ocean because the Japanese Current comes into the area around Kodiak. It is considered warmer than some of the other areas, but Kathy found it too cold.

When boats were emptied of their catches, Kathy and her close friend would clean them to earn money.

It was the custom to give priests from the sea's "first catch" and invite them to everything—including the yearly Alaskan King Crab Festival. It was the first opportunity for Kathy to see a five- foot-seven- inch span of a crab when she was there. She was amazed

Kathy liked to go down the hill to the movies and occasionally her *babushka* Xenia, would go with her. One time they came home after a movie to an unbelievable scene: huge pots and pans were everywhere; big, live crabs were moving all over the place in water that Roman had slopped onto the floor. Xenia was horrified.

"Oh, just don't worry about it," Roman said.

Xenia's response was, "Didn't they bring them to you cooked?"

Roman confessed to asking them to bring them to him raw! He wanted to try his hand at cooking them. This brought on a heated exchange between Roman and Xenia which continued in several languages while Kathy looked on in amusement. Xenia explained to Kathy that this was the way Russians talked. But, by now, Kathy understood most of what they were saying!

Finally, Xenia grabbed Kathy and said, "We're leaving." Then she said in an aside to Roman, "This had better be clean by the time we get home." As they marched out the door, they gave one last look to the water, mess, and crabs and shook their heads.

After the movie, when Xenia and Kathy got home they saw that Roman had attempted to clean up the mess. It wasn't really great, but he'd done what he could. The kitchen didn't bother Xenia too much because she had never really learned how to cook—and Xenia never taught daughter Natalie, either—she would rather read. That meant Roman had to contend.

Those crabs crawling in the kitchen could easily have represented several weeks' worth of food for a family. One immense leg alone would make a nice meal.

Other foods and cattle were raised on the mainland where Kodiak bears were dangerous and a threat to the cattle. One time Kathy visited another friend at their farm and went riding bareback when the horse sensed a bear and took off for home. "I had to hold on like mad to keep from flying off," Kathy told Xenia.

One of Kodiak's publications called Father Sturmer "a popular priest; a Kodiak living legend". He was known for his insight, humor and his delight at visiting with everyone. Both he and Xenia loved the Russian atmosphere of Kodiak: the culture and the language reminded them so much of their homeland they'd longed for. But, likewise, being so family oriented, they continued to miss their children and grandchildren. They longed to be with them and decided it was time to leave their home here. Only this time, they were leaving by choice.

In 1961, Father Sturmer was chosen to become Dean at Holy Trinity Cathedral in San Francisco, within easier reach of the family. Once again they were blessed.

Looking every bit the part of the priest, a serious-faced, Father Roman Sturmer with his dark rimmed glasses hiding the twinkle in his eyes, a hefty stature, and a flowing, square-cut gray beard returned with his delightful, witty, ever-supportive wife, *Babushka* Xenia to the Bay Area.

Once again they could visit their beloved family and many of their old Russian friends. Generally, these gatherings were very large as the grandchildren now numbered ten. Alex's and Natalie's families each had five children. Church holidays are an important part of the Orthodox religion and the family loved to be together at these times.

As Roman and Xenia looked back, despite the tragedies and losses, they had been miraculously protected.

Roman's heartfelt desire to serve God as a priest had been fulfilled with Xenia by his side.

Once again, they had been privileged to enjoy the customs of their culture in an atmosphere similar in many ways, to their beloved Russia.

Now they would bask in family love.

They were content.

Mathew 10:29-31 English Standard Version (ESV),

Are not two sparrows sold for a penny? And not one of them will fall to the ground apart from your Father. But even the hairs on your head are all numbered. Fear not, therefore; you are of more value than many sparrows.

Epilogue

In October, 1972, Roman and Xenia celebrated their fiftieth wedding anniversary. The gathering turned out to be so large the party had to move to the cafeteria at the Pleasanton Fairgrounds. It was a joyous time as many stories were shared. Roman and Xenia had a wonderful time re-living their experiences.

Roman retired and they moved to Santa Barbara. Once again they missed the family and admonished them often for not calling.

Due to illness, Father Sturmer and Xenia moved to Pleasanton in 1978 to live with Alex, Millie, and their children. Roman died of cancer on February 4, 1979.

Matushka Xenia Sturmer, deciding to exert her independence at last, moved to her own apartment in Berkeley where she continued to visit with family and friends there. She discovered soap operas on television, but continued to read many books. She died on April 11, 1987 of a heart attack.

J & P Oliver

Authors' Biography

The Evicted was co-authored by John and Patricia Oliver over a period of many years. The late John Oliver personally knew the elder Sturmers and spent many hours interviewing Roman prior to Roman's death. Together, both John and Patty interviewed family members and were provided with much material. Even through a loss of eyesight and failing health, John had a passion for completing this story and fulfilling a promise to the Sturmer family.

John Oliver was a well-known columnist, editor and freelance writer for over thirty years. For many years, he worked for *The Tri-Valley Herald*, a large newspaper chain in the California Bay Area. He authored numerous articles and feature stories, including one for *People* magazine, as well as two books for Logos. One book, *Eldridge Cleaver Reborn*, a full accounting of the former Black Panther leader, was based on face-to-face interviews.

Until John's death in 2014, John and Patricia collaborated on this biography and other writing endeavors. Patricia, also a published writer, spent years in the business world utilizing her love of writing. She diligently did much research on *The Evicted* in addition to writing; she has completed the project as was promised.

GLOSSARY:

Alexander III
   Ship renamed by the Bolsheviks to the *Volya.*
Alexsandrowicz, Edmund (Eddie)
   Natalie Sturmer's first husband.
Alexeyevich, Pyotr
   Czar of Russia, known as Peter the Great.
Bilibid Prison
   The "new" prison in Manila where Bataan prisoners were taken.
Bolshevik.
   "The Reds", Lenin and Trotsky were at the nation's helm.
Brest-Litovsk Treaty
   Treaty signed on March 3, 1918 between Soviet Russia and
   Central Powers marking the   exit of Russia's part in WWI.
Charnetsky, Ladislaus
   A good friend of Roman Sturmer.
Denikin, Anton Ivanovich
   Lieutenant General of the Imperial Russian Army in 1916 and
   one of the generals of the Whites during the Russian Civil War.
Dobriansky, Mitrophan
   Xenia's grandfather on mother's side.
Dobriansky, Nadejhda1
   A Russian noblewoman, mother of Xenia Harvey.
Domanski, Vicente
   The Sturmer family chef.
Duma Government
   An elected semi-representative body in **Russia** from 1906 to
   1917.
Von Eichorn, Hermann
   German Field Marshal.
Empress Catherine the Great
   Roman's second ship renamed the *Svobodnaya Rossiia.*
Empress Maria
   Roman's first ship.

Eustacius
> A smaller ship.

Fock, Volodya
> A seaman and Roman's close friend/

Gdansk
> Poland's harbor on the Baltic Sea.

Hamel, Bert
> Second husband of Natasha "Tassie" Alexandrowicz.

Harvey, Nicholas
> Xenia's father; a British subject and editor of a British paper in Moscow, *Otro Russii.*

Harvey, Xenia
> A young woman in love with Roman.

Kerensky, Alexander
> A member of the Duma government.

Kolchak, Alexander V.
> A Russian naval commander and explorer in charge of the anti-Communist White forces during the Russian Civil War.

Kornilov, Lavr G.
> A military intelligence officer and General in the Imperial Russian Army during World   War I and Russian Civil War.

Kuznetsky, Capt.
> Ordered Roman off *Catherine the Great* ship.

Levgovd, Lt.
> A friend of Roman.

MacArthur, Douglas
> A General, and Military Advisor to the Philippines.

Nasarjhevsky, Kazimir
> Inna's father and Roman's grandfather (*Dedushka.*).

Order of St. Anna
> The Russian medal of honor given for bravery.

Petrograd
> Formally St. Petersburg.

Petrograd Women's Medical Institute
> An exceptional school, founded in 1897 and reputed to be the

first Russian higher medical school especially for women.

Pokrovsky, Andriy
  Admiral was a three-star officer, Admiral of Nikolayev.

Rasputin
  An evil peasant believed to have healing powers.

Sablin, Mikhail Pavlovich-An admiral in the Imperial Russian Navy and
  a member of the White Russian Movement.

Santo Tomás
  One of the oldest universities in the Philippines, located in
  Manilla.

Sturmer, Arcady
  Roman's father and a Colonel in the Russian army.

Sturmer, Inna Nasarjhevsky
  Roman's mother.

Oleg, George, & Kira
  Roman's siblings.

Sturmer, Roman
  A Lieutenant in the Royal Navy who later became a priest.

Tzaritzin &Kamyshin
  Oil distribution centers of the Volga region.

Utro Rossii
  'Russia's Morning', name of Xenia Harvey's father's newspaper.

Vantz, Herbert
  Chairman of a ship's committee.

Wood, Leonard
  The U.S. Governor-General of the Philippines.

Wrangel, Baron Pyotr N.
  An officer in the Imperial Russian army and later commanding
  General of the anti-Bolshevik White Army in Southern Russia
  in the later stages of the Russian Civil War.

Zolotuhin, Peter
  A friend of Roman Sturmer and Volodya Fock.

WARS:

*The **Russian Revolution of 1905*** was said to be a major factor to the February Revolutions of 1917. The events of Bloody Sunday triggered a line of protests. A council of workers called the St. Petersburg Soviet was created in all this chaos, and the beginning of a communist political protest had begun.

Russia's Great War & Revolution, 1914-1922. A collective term of a series of revolutions in which the Czarist autocracy was toppled in 1917.

*The **Great War*** was the WWI, 1914-1918 and part of Russia's revolution.

*The **Russian Civil War**, **1918 - 1923*** was a multi-party war in the former Russian Empire fought between the Bolshevik Red Army and the White Army, the loosely allied anti-Bolshevik forces.

Order of St. Anna, 3rd class

Made in the USA
Las Vegas, NV
21 March 2022

46058875R00148